MERCHANTS

OF

MISERY

AUTHORS AGAINST ADDICTION

MERCHANTS

OF

MISERY

edited by Lisa Dabrowski & L. Joseph Shosty

Merchants of Misery
edited by Lisa Dabrowski & L. Joseph Shosty

ISBN: 0692977627
ISBN-13: 978-0692977620

For Robyn, Jes, and Chloe--LD

For William--LJS

Contents

Foreword

According to DrugAbuse.gov, *"Addiction is a chronic, often relapsing brain disease that causes compulsive drug seeking and use, despite harmful consequences to the addicted individual and to those around him or her...But addiction is characterized by the inability to stop. Jun 30, 2016"*

This is the clinical definition of Addiction given by the Government. I have some personal experience with Addiction and Addicts. They often start off using Opiate Pain Killers prescribed legally by their physicians, become hooked and progress to street drugs such as Heroin. They will do anything to get a fix. Is it because they are evil, rotten criminals? No. It is because when the heroin wears off they have flu like symptoms, and they will do anything to avoid that sickness. They ARE Sick, PERIOD. They need help. Most Addicts don't enjoy the lives they are living, often losing everything valuable to them: homes, families, jobs, children. They need help.

There is help available to them, but one factor that often impedes their recovery is lack of funding to treatment centers, sober houses, and recovery centers.

Once an addict admits defeat, if he is lucky enough to make it that far, he must make a complete surrender. It is vital that he admits that he is powerless over his Addiction and his life is unmanageable. It is with this first step that he can begin his road to recovery.

On a personal note, it's easy just to call addicts Junkies, but when you do remember that the Junkie you are talking about is someone's son, daughter, brother, sister, mother or father. They are not just Junk, they are Human Beings who are waging a War on Drugs.

Thank you for taking the time to read this, and to help out someone suffering from Addiction.

Lisa Dabrowski

Merchants of Misery

Lisa Dabrowski

Preying upon his sickness
I feed his hunger in increments
Miniscule doses until it grows
Into an insatiable mindless beast
He is in MY power now
Utterly helpless and hopeless
The victim of his own demise
Weaved into a Maddening Web
Bought with his heart and soul
From The Merchant of Misery

Fleurs du Mal

Edward Ahern

Jamie swallowed the dregs from the bottle of wine he'd opened an hour earlier, then spoke.

"I wish you still drank. You were less serious."

Paul snorted. "Don't keep flogging the same ex-drunk. You know I had to stop. I'm headed home. If you remember, tell Claudia I said good night."

"I sometimes think the only reason you still come over here is so you can look at her."

"I sometimes think you're right."

Jamie heaved out of his chair. "Agh, Paul, God damn it, stay; you're the only person I can open up to."

"We'll talk when you're sober. I'm home tomorrow if you want to stop by."

Paul's bachelor-sized cape cod was two blocks from Jamie's house. The atomized effect of Jamie's wine lingered on his skin. I wonder, he thought as he backtracked home, if I took a sip by osmosis.

The next morning, Paul was halfway through his second cup of coffee when the mail flap on the front door chattered. He scooped up the printed flotsam, walked over to the waste basket, and began throwing pieces away.

He was near the bottom of the stack when an envelope caught his attention, one written in heavy script and sealed with grape-purple wax. Paul Freeman. He broke the seal and pulled out a card twice the thickness of the envelope.

"Mr. Paul Freeman and one guest are invited to sample the most recent bottling of Fleurs du Mal. The tasting will be on the twelfth day of June, at seven o'clock in the evening. Arrangements have been made to take Mr. Freeman and guest at six o'clock in the evening from his domicile to the vignoble.

Hermes Treblewise"

The invitation was absurd. He'd never heard of Fleurs du Mal, and anyone who knew him knew he didn't drink anymore. But the paper quality was better than any wedding invitation Paul had ever received. He carried the invitation and a coffee refill with him into his backyard garden.

An hour later, Jamie's apologies preceded him into the yard.

"Jesus, Paul, I'm sorry. I'm getting to be a weekend wino. Whatever I said, I didn't mean it..."

Paul sighed as Jamie emerged through the garden gate. "I can't figure out why Claudia stays with you. It's sure as hell not your drunken charm. You need to quit before it gets serious."

Jamie tensed, then relaxed. "We can't all be abstainers like you."

He dropped into a lawn chair next to Paul and noticed the invitation. "Wow. Nice paper. Hand laid linen, I think. See the wire marks? And the ink. Looks almost medieval. Did you know they used to make ink from dried hawthorn branches or pounded gallnut? This has got that same gray-brown tint to it."

"And how the hell do you know this?"

"I'm not your editor for nothing. Just for pitifully little. But I do know about paper and ink. Fleurs du Mal? I've heard hints about it. It's a liquor. Never sold commercially, doled out a bottle at a time to the select few. You've got to go!"

"I've got to not go. I'm a drunk, remember? You of all people don't want me acting like I used to."

"Yeah, but still, it says 'and friend.' You could take me, and I'll make sure you don't drink."

"It's got to be a mistake. I'd call and tell them, but there's no phone number or address."

Jamie slowly waved the invitation. "Aren't you curious? About how you got picked? About Hermes and his booze? You don't have to drink; I'll tell you about it."

"Just what I'm afraid of."

"Look, if you get goosy, start feeling trapped, I'll pay for a taxi home. We can't pass up this chance."

"We? Watch me."

He walked Jamie back over to his house and said hello to Claudia. Paul wanted to touch her, but didn't. Her leggy angularity was filling out nicely as she approached forty.

She showed up at his house an hour later. "Jamie's mad that you're not taking him to a wine tasting."

"Hi, Claudia. That's poignantly tough shit, but your softening me up isn't going to change my mind. I'd go with you--you'd stay sober enough to make sure I didn't drink."

Claudia threw a well-remembered gaze at him.

"It's a big deal to him, Paul. You said your sobriety is pretty solid." She crossed her legs.

Paul's lips pursed. She'd always known how to barrage his senses. "It's a bad idea. You shouldn't beg for him."

"It's not like that, Paul. It's just that what's important to him is important for me, too."

Paul shrugged. "All right. All right. For old times' sake. I should be able to survive for three hours. Tell Jamie we'll go."

For the next several days Paul resumed ghost writing the autobiography of a completely self-absorbed tech executive and dithering about whether he should dress up or down for his visit to Treblewise. *If I dress up, it seems important. Casual, it is.* His AA sponsor had been adamant about his not going. But for the first time, Paul had balked against his instructions. It seemed important to prove his sobriety.

Jamie and Paul's ride that Saturday evening was a black town car with darkened windows. The burly driver said he knew nothing other than the address, and that the trip would take less than an hour.

During the ride, Jaime chattered nonstop about research he'd done on Treblewise and Fleurs du Mal, and what a privilege the visit was. Paul answered in monosyllables, distracted by the pending assault on his sobriety.

They stepped out of the car to face two stories of roughly dressed, quarter-ton stones topped with a slate roof. The narrow, deep-set windows were confined by black iron bars. Planted fields and hot houses surrounded the building. Paul recognized mountain laurel and lilies, daffodils and philodendron, Scotch broom and hemlock, but several hundred more species grew and flowered under glass panes or out in the open fields.

The driver told them he would return in two hours to drive them home. They crunched their way along a gravel walkway to a deeply inset door of thick wood slabs. Paul thought he saw oleander in one of the hot houses, and milkweed and bloodroot growing along the verge.

Jamie bounced with excitement. "This place looks like a little castle."

"Or a dungeon. It must be clammy as hell in there."

The door opened to their first knocking. "Mr. Freeman. How I've anticipated your coming. And this is?"

"Jamie Carrington, my neighbor."

"And your editor, I believe."

Hermes Treblewise's gauntness was masked under a black robe. The stubble on the top of his head advised that his monk's pate was self-inflicted rather than genetic. His eyes were the color of mouse fur, indistinctly gray/brown. His handshake was aridly hot.

"Mr. Treblewise, I have to tell you from the onset that I no longer drink alcohol."

"Brother Treblewise, please. I knew that when I sent you the invitation, Mr. Freeman. But your prior reputation as a wine taster precedes you. I think you'll find my Fleurs du Mal interesting."

"Not anymore."

"Wait until you hear about it."

The monk ushered them into a study. They sat in

armchairs facing a stone fireplace. Inscribed stone slabs covered the floor, and the inside walls were the same rough dressed stones as the outside. Despite the fire, the room was dank.

An ornate crest filled the wall above the fireplace mantel. Jamie tried to read the Latin lettering. "Tramagist? No, that's not right. Trismagistus I think."

"Very good, Mr. Carrington. It's an obsolete spelling of my last name. Mr. Freeman, you're a gardener and amateur horticulturalist, so you'll appreciate my explanation.

"Some while ago I joined the Benedictine order and became one of their herbologists and vignerons…"

Jamie interjected. "Are you still Benedictine? I didn't notice any crosses in your house."

"Ah, no, regrettably my studies diverged from their requirements, and I established my own little order. But no matter." Hermes crossed his legs. His feet were shod in open-toed sandals. His toenails were completely black and snipped straight across.

"I wished to produce a liquor from flowers and berries. But not just some sickly-sweet grape brandy. I wanted to produce an elixir, a tonic that would make one drunk if enough was consumed, but in moderation would give a man heightened sensitivities.

"There was no point in distilling from the usual suspects: pears or cherries or cloudberries. They'd all been used and only succeeded in getting one tipsy and sugar-overdosed.

"No, I went further afield, finding flowers and berries previously ignored or detested. My initial efforts had unfortunate consequences, but I persevered."

Treblewise paused. "I'm being ill mannered. Would you care for a glass of wine? The grapes are cultivated here at the vignoble."

Jamie answered without pause. "Yes, please. Is this the Fleurs du Mal?"

"Ah, no, just our *vin du table*. And you Mr. Freeman?"

"I won't insult you by asking for a soft drink. Just water please."

Paul was interested despite himself. "So, the plants and shrubs we saw on the way in are used for the Fleurs du Mal?"

"Yes. Each vintage is prepared to achieve a somewhat different effect, and the exact ingredients vary from year to year, to suit the intended drinkers."

Jamie finished off his glass of wine before Paul was halfway through his water. Treblewise poured Jamie another glass without asking.

"So, Mr. Freeman. Your prior achievements as an oenophile are the reason you received the invitation. A few small sips of Fleurs du Mal will enhance your senses and awareness far beyond your most lucid moments. Great things have been done while under its influence. I would very much like for you to vary slightly from your non-use of alcohol and provide me with a report based on your educated palate."

The flattery was sinuous. Paul had written books about wines and cordials. Curiosity tugged at his taste buds. "I'm sorry, Brother Treblewise, but I can't do that. I am curious, though; how did you decide to call this liquor Fleurs du Mal?"

Treblewise visibly swallowed his displeasure at

the refusal, then regained his manners. "Ah, yes, it's taken from a collection of poems by Charles Baudelaire. Do you read him? No? One of the poems in his book, 'Fleurs du Mal' is about a monk. The last two stanzas in English would go something like:

> *'My soul's a tomb, which-wretched friar!-I*
> *Have paced since time began, and occupy:*
> *Bare walled and hateful still my cloister stands.*

> *'O slothful monk! When shall I learn to make*
> *In the stark drama of a living mind*
> *My special joy and work to fit my hands'.*

"I think Baudelaire describes me well."

Jamie had been silent witness to the byplay. "But, Paul, surely in such small quantities you could provide an evaluation?"

Paul glowered. "No way in hell."

Treblewise studied them both and shrugged. "Well, Mr. Carrington. I believe you are also familiar with wines and spirits, although perhaps not with quite the discerning palate of Mr. Freeman. How would it be if I were to give you a bottle of Fleurs du Mal for your tasting?"

"Absolutely!"

Treblewise turned to Paul. "I ask only that you observe the liquor's effect on Mr. Carrington and report back to me."

Jamie also turned his head toward Paul. "Please, Paul. You won't be tasting, just watching me drink, like you always do."

"Well, hell, all right, as long as I don't have to drink. How often do I have to report?"

"Once a week should do. I have no phone or internet, so you'll have to report in person. The driver will pick you up each week."

Treblewise left and returned with a green bottle. There was no label. He carefully opened the bottle with a bone-handled corkscrew, poured out a half ounce of the liquor and held it out.

"Mr. Carrington, would you please affirm that you are accepting this libation of your own free will, without inducement or threat?"

"Yes, yes, of course."

As Jamie held the snifter before drinking, Treblewise continued. "The changes in your aptitudes and moods will be profound, Mr. Carrington. You'll literally become a different man. The effect will be both liberating and intoxicating. I'm required to warn you that overindulgence is quite dangerous. That's why you, Mr. Freeman, will be the one reporting back to me."

Paul visualized the white oleander he'd seen in the garden, and realized that every flower and herb he'd just seen were in some way poisonous. If Jaime drank too much of this potion, he'd suffer much worse than a hangover. And Jaime needed baby-sitting.

"Don't do it, Jamie. Just put it down, and we'll go home."

Jamie stared down at the minute amount of liquor in the snifter. "I could survive drinking this much paint thinner." He put his nose over the crystal and sniffed. "Wow. Really complex, Paul. I don't sense the alcohol, just flowers and berries."

He took a tiny sip and rolled it around his tongue and back onto his palette. He breathed several times through his nose. "It's like nothing else I've ever drunk. It's--I have no comparison, Paul. It's like drinking flower petals from an exotic garden. My tongue has opened up. I think I can taste my own saliva."

Treblewise's mouth squirmed into a smile meant only for himself. "Remember my warning, Mr. Carrington. Don't drink any more for some days. And now, my good souls, your driver has arrived. Mr. Freeman, he'll pick you up at the same time next week? Detailed notes and descriptions, please."

The return trip was spent largely in silence. Jamie cradled the bottle, self-absorbed in new sensations. Paul wallowed in drunkard's remorse without knowing why he should feel guilty. "Jamie, don't drink any more of that stuff. I'll give him back the bottle next week."

"No way, Paul. I think my hormones just kicked into an overdrive I haven't felt since high school. And my vision seems sharper."

"At least let me do some homework on this before you suck down another shot."

"Yeah, okay, sure." But Jamie was already distracted, waving his fingers in front of his face as if fascinated by vapor trails.

When the car dropped him home, Paul marched directly from his front door to the computer. Two hours later he called Jamie, but got Claudia.

"Claudia, how is he?"

"Fine, I guess. He's just had another snifter from the green bottle and seems hyper-elated. Not drunk, but really wired."

"Jesus, put him on please."

There was a scuffling noise which sounded like

Jamie pulling the phone from Claudia's hand. "Paul, it's incredible. I can almost taste colors. And I've thought my way out of a couple crappy problems at work. This stuff is the elixir of life."

"Like hell, it is. Listen to me. Fleurs du Mal doesn't mean bad flowers. It means flowers of evil. Every one of those plants we saw on the way in and out has poisonous flowers and berries. Every one. You're drinking poison. Dump it out."

"In your dreams, Paul. Except for a few minutes of my honeymoon, I've never felt this good. And it's continuous. The second slug only made it better, stronger."

"Second? Listen to me. For God's sake, throw the shit away. Just save me a little so I can get it analyzed."

"Too late for you. buddy. No sips for you, just for me."

"Put Claudia back on...Claudia? Don't let him touch that stuff again. I don't know what the hell we've gotten into, but I think that crap could kill him."

"He is different, Paul. More demanding. More self-absorbed. But he's not drunk, and he doesn't look poisoned."

Paul started out the door for a return to Treblewise's stone fortress, but realized he had no idea of the routing they'd taken, just vague images filtered through the darkened glass of the limo. After an hour's dithering, he walked over to Jamie's house. Claudia answered the door bell. She had hand-sized welts on her arms.

"He's not here, Paul. He took a third sip and left. I tried to stop him, but..." She waved her bruised arms. "I couldn't stop him. I don't know where he went." She started crying, soundlessly and without affectation.

Paul cupped her elbows and steered her back inside, sitting next to her on the sofa. He held her in silence for several minutes. "Where's the bottle, Claudia?"

"Jamie took it with him. He's like he used to get after snorting coke. His mind is racing so fast, I don't think he can apply the brakes. He-he said things to me, Paul. And did things. Creepy, hurtful things. And I think he meant them."

"He loves you, Claudia, we know that. This damn liquor has short-circuited him. Did he take his cell phone?"

"Yes, but he told me not to call."

"I'll try and call him later."

Paul held her again, and this time Claudia put her arms around him. When the fading dusk had completely died, he shifted to face her and kissed her gently on the lips. It was as good as he remembered.

"Once I find him, I'll break the bottle. I'm stronger than he is. Call me as soon as he gets back, and I'll come over."

He called Jamie after reaching home, but was dumped into voice mail.

"Jamie, for Christ's sake, pick up. You've scared the shit out of Claudia and got me really worried. Call me as soon as you get this, no matter what time it is."

Paul fired up the desk top and went into search mode on Hermes Treblewise, but got nowhere. Then he remembered Jamie's reading of the emblem in Treblewise's living room. Trismas? No, no Trismagistus. Lots on that son of a bitch. A legendary alchemist, drummed out of the Catholic Church several hundred years ago. He'd tried to develop an elixir of life from death dealing plants, once poisoning off thirty of his followers with the assurance that they would be able to see God. And so they did, once they'd died.

And this crazy pseudo monk is just as medieval as his namesake.

Paul called Jamie a little after 1a.m. and left another message, then went to bed. His cell phone went off two hours later.

"My eyes have seen such glories, Paul."

"Where are you, Jamie?"

"I'm riding a celestial dragon. Fleurs du Mal! It's a tree of knowledge."

"Jamie, I can pick you up. Where are you?"

"I'm not going back to what I was. Oh, and Paul. You and Claudia. Take care of her. I told her you would."

"You're drunk."

"No, my friend, I'm lucent. The clarity is so piercing, it hurts my bones."

The phone went dead. Paul redialed without success. The next morning, he drove over and picked up Claudia. They spent the day walking through neighborhoods Jamie had once frequented to score drugs. Paul found himself twisting between fear for Jamie and perverse enjoyment of the time spent with Claudia. When he dropped her off, she started crying again. Paul hugged her tightly, vainly trying to squeeze in relief from her pain.

The next three days spiraled identically. They called Jamie's friends and fellow editors, police and hospitals in the morning, and in the afternoon and evening prowled unlikely places where he might have secreted himself.

The reassurance of words failed them, and they increasingly just touched and held each other. Paul kissed her morning and evening, his best pledge that she wasn't at fault and was still loved.

The hospital called the day before Treblewise's limo was scheduled to arrive. Jamie had washed ashore. They were at the intensive care ward within twenty minutes, and fifteen minutes after that were listening to the young ER doctor.

"Mrs. Carrington, Jamie is dangerously ill. We're flushing out his system, but our toxicology results are still coming back with dangerously high levels of various poisons. In his lucid moments, he's told us this was self-administered through some kind of drink. Is this true?"

"Yes, doctor. Did they find a bottle with him when he was found?"

"According to police he put up quite a fight when they took it away from him. Which is odd because it was empty. We have him under suicide watch."

"Sweet Jesus," Paul blurted out, "he drank it all. But you're purging him?"

"Like I said. Um, Mrs. Carrington, he asked that you not be admitted to his room, but that he be awakened as soon as Mr. Freeman arrived. Are there domestic issues we should be aware of?"

Claudia's face, swollen from crying, congealed into lumpiness. She sobbed but didn't cry again. "Does he look that bad?"

Paul interrupted. "Doctor, tell Jamie that I'll see him with Claudia or not at all."

The doctor left to talk to Jaime, and returned five minutes later. "He'll see you both." The doctor lead Paul and Claudia down a corridor lined on both sides with gurneys occupied by patients in visible pain.

Jamie's appearance was even worse than expected. The poisons had sprouted open sores on his face and arms, and presumably over the rest of his body as well. His eyes were the yellow of liver failure. He looked gaunt, but his mood was aggressive.

"Paul, when you see Treblewise tomorrow, tell him I need two bottles this time."

Claudia started to cry, but Jamie ignored her, staring intently at Paul.

"Jamie, I'm not going back to Treblewise's, and I'm sure as hell not getting you any more of that liquor."

Jamie began to shake. "It's an all-knowing, cosmic firework, Paul. I'm willing to flame out quickly. Just don't make me die in withdrawal."

"You're not going to die, but I hope you suffer like hell."

Jamie half-flopped out of the bed, clutching at Paul. An orderly grabbed him and held him down on the bed.

"Restraints, doctor?"

"Yes, they're indicated."

Claudia and Paul ate in the hospital cafeteria and drove back to her house. No conversation. No music. Paul found a bottle of wine, opened it, and brought her a glass. "It's not very good."

"I don't care. Paul, you have to go see that monk tomorrow."

"Not a chance."

"No, listen. If anyone knows what the antidote

might be, he would. You have to ask him."

Paul poured her a second glass. They talked of minute, safe things. He leaned forward and kissed her again, not good night. Old memories took hold, and then resurged into familiar rhythms. Paul spent the night.

Over breakfast the next morning they talked as if long married--of tending to Jamie, of Paul's trip to see the monk, their intimacy stored away in a curio cabinet.

The stoic limousine driver was punctual. Paul tried to question him about the address of the vignoble, about its direction, but the driver held silent. Once inside the limo Paul noticed that the screen dividing him and the driver and the side and rear windows were almost completely opaque. Had they been this way before? Paul cursed his inattentiveness. If he had been more aware, if he had only sensed the inherent malevolence of the invitation, perhaps Jamie wouldn't be in the state he was in. As they started off he pulled his cell phone. It gave him an immediate error message, not even recognizing his current location.

Next time I have somebody follow us, he thought, though he doubted if there would be a next time.

Treblewise again answered the first knock. Paul exploded before he stepped into the building. "Jamie's poisoned, maybe dying. You gave a drunk an alcoholic poison. I'm going to have you arrested."

"Ah, Mr. Freeman. Please do come in so we can speak in comfort."

Paul continued to storm as he drew inside. "You made this crap. What can he take to counteract its effects?"

The monk stood there regarding Paul with a serene expression, arms folded into the voluminous sleeves of his robe.

"Nothing. However, the effects of a bottle of Fleurs du Mal drank over several days might not kill him. A second bottle, drunk quickly, would assuredly be painfully fatal. I have two more bottles here."

"That he'll never get."

Treblewise's eyes developed a mustard tinge. "Don't be obtuse, Mr. Freeman. Mr. Carrington is nothing special to me, just another tippler. You, however, roused my attention. You were a discerning taster and critic before you dried out and detoured.

"I'll offer you a choice, Mr. Freeman. I'll ensure that Mr. Carrington is never able to again drink Fleurs du Mal if you agree to sample it. I'll pour you a drollop here, and you take a bottle back with you. Mr. Carrington will probably recover, although I expect he'll be scarred and bitter. You'd just have to control the liquor and its visions."

"Go to hell. I'll never drink again. And I'll make sure that Jamie doesn't, either."

"You know better. My driver is extraordinarily devoted. He'll have no trouble getting a bottle into Mr. Carrington's willing hands. Think, Mr. Freeman. Is your threatened sobriety worth his assured death?"

"I'm not going to be blackmailed into being my brother's keeper."

"Very well, Mr. Freeman, since that's your final answer." Treblewise grinned. "Welcome back. Mr. and Mrs. Carrington can be told whatever you wish."

"Welcome back?"

"Envy, pride, lust--more than adequate, and in only a few days. John 15:13, Mr. Freeman. Au revoir.

We'll meet again."

The driver had silently entered the room. Paul wanted to wrestle Treblewise to the ground, but the driver would have beaten him down before he could accomplish anything. Treblewise smiled paternally as Paul raged out of the building.

Paul demanded the driver drop him at Claudia's. He shook with alternating surges of anger and fear the whole way.

Claudia was waiting for him. "Did you get an antidote?"

"No. We're going to have to guard Jamie. Treblewise will try and supply him with the liquor."

"Can we go to the police?"

"We wouldn't be believed, and there's nothing we could tell them that would help them find Treblewise. We have to get through this together." Paul put his arm gently around Claudia's waist and guided her back into the house. Shortly after midnight he got up, went to Claudia's computer and plugged in John 15:13. He could hear Treblewise mouthing the words.

"Greater love has no one than this, that he lay down his life for his friends."

Paul stared without focus. *How the hell do I keep a raving addict away from his dealer? And even if I'm able to cut him off from his drug of choice, won't he just switch back to booze and drink himself to death? And why do I warrant Treblewise's attention?*

Claudia appeared in the doorway, eyes bleary with sleep yet hair tousled and achingly beautiful. "Are you coming back to bed?"

I wonder, he thought, *if Adam and Eve would have also suffered by not eating the fruit.*
"Yes."

A Dusty Road Wedding

Eddie Generous

Sometimes, history has a hard time letting go, it sticks around awhile, and there's nothing you can do but stay out of its way.

I've learned this the hard way.

~/~

It was sunny and hot, the breeze combed through the hair on the top of my head. The car was new, new to me, a trade-in I couldn't help but pounce on. My wife was in a mood, so I hadn't told her I'd actually bought the car. Instead, I said it was trade-in in need of a test drive. As usual, she greyed when I got into shoptalk. I continued talking because I knew something she didn't know I knew.

There was an affair.

I'd installed a baby-monitoring camera in the

bedroom.

I had her dead to rights.

My squeaky new lawyer suggested I keep things on the level until we slammed the paperwork on her. See, I worked longer hours, but I made less money, and dammit, I was accustomed to a certain style of existence.

~/~

The camera was set on sound and motion. My eyes slid to the old CRT monitor on my desk when the red icon blipped, and my wife brought the too-damned-young man into our room. The hairs on the back of my neck rose like the guy's hands, working her shirt free over her head. He sucked on her nipples through her bra, and I clenched my fists. I imagined taking a tire iron to the camera and everything it saw. I closed my eyes and saw the motion in shady silhouettes. I shook my head and heard the wet smacks of the in-and-out. I opened my eyes, and her head tilted back while she rode him. I remembered that response.

How long had it been since we shared something so honest?

A woman came into the dealership while I watched the tiny screen at the corner of my monitor, a furious, uncomfortable erection demanding I destroy something. I wasn't in the mood to stand and shake, but I closed the video on the monitor. I was distracted and uncaring as she introduced herself and announced she had a car to trade.

It wasn't until I saw the ride that I slipped from misery mode to smooth as grease mode. My urges transformed, and I stood embarrassment-free.

We had this showpiece BMW out front, and she wanted it. My belly did barrel rolls; selling a car like that comes with mondo commission. She hated the shiny Chevelle she'd driven onto the lot. It was bad on gas, she said. It didn't have Bluetooth. It didn't have air conditioning. The only perk messed up her hair. It was her ex-husband's car anyway; she'd taken it in the divorce out of spite.

"I can't give you much. The market for older cars isn't what it once was," I said, which was true, but the market had been making a strong comeback, and this Chevelle was the jelly in a morning doughnut.

"Don't care. I want the fancy one out there."

I ran my finger on the red pin stripe. "I can knock two-grand off the price. Like you said, this one's a guzzler."

The woman shrugged. Divorce car, divorce money: it was all gravy to her. All gravy to me, too. We were basically a pair of baked potatoes swimming in easy decisions.

~/~

"A great day for a wedding," I said, looking out the window. I wore my salesman's grin to ward off the grimace fighting to acknowledge that my marriage to Jenny was a lemon.

The wedding was more than an hour's drive, out in the boonies on a reformed cattle farm. There was a map on the back of the invitation, but it wasn't great. She didn't put down the physical coordinates, killing the option of putting the address into my phone's GPS.

I wore my blue suit, the one I wore for weddings, as opposed to the black suit I reserved for funerals. The black one would've been more befitting for this wedding, but I'm climbing ahead.

Jenny wore a pink and blue dress. We looked pretty good standing side-by-side in the mirror. It threw an achy curveball into my stomach. I knew I was going to miss the girl I'd married, way back when she'd loved me and I'd loved her. Not that either of us were all that young when we wed. I was thirty, and she was twenty-seven. At the time we'd seemed old enough to make a wise decision.

Turns out there are no wise decisions when it comes to love.

Feeling the power around me pushed my mood for the better, and I blazed a dusty trail over the gravel road, humming along with the AM country station the most recent owner had the dial set to. By my calculations, we should've met with the balloons at the end of a laneway by now.

"Do you think we missed it?" asked Jenny.

"Hope not. Why the old farm, anyway?"

"The groom's some kind of history buff. Something happened at the farm. I don't remember. Some kind of murder, or something. Doesn't matter if we miss the ceremony..."

"Cool down, we'll get there. It doesn't kick off for another thirty minutes, and you know they never start on-time," I said, thinking sometimes they did. It was rare, but not unheard of, and then I wondered if making her late for a wedding might be one of those things lawyers use in an argument.

The radio hissed and spat a horrid mash of static and signal. It went on for twenty seconds before the dial settled and a crackly voice explained that pork prices were down again.

Two cents a pound?

I turned it up. Jenny started into me again, and I missed the rest of the trade report. An old song spun through the speakers.

"We're going to be late, and it's your fault. You're so stupid you can't even follow a simple map, and you had to take this mid-life crisis mobile. You're always bringing me down."

I tried to ignore her and stared blankly at the radio, listening to the ancient jam. Just then the road veered, and I didn't. The right front drove over the grass, and I immediately straightened. Too late, a snake hissed from the driver's side tire. Jenny screamed.

Stockpiling my emotions all week left me muddled. I tossed my jacket into the backseat and opened the trunk. It was empty, not even a hideaway hump.

"No spare," I said and pulled my phone from my pocket. No bars. "Do you have any service?"

"Ugh, you asshole." She looked at her phone. "I just had serv...Oh, hello there," she said looking past me.

There was a small boy in a straw hat and baggy pants, his boots a few sizes too big, behind me and to the right. He'd crept up behind us to stare at the car, or so I figured. He looked like a bumpkin from a depression era film.

"Hello, boy, do you know where I might find a telephone?" I asked.

The boy gave a curious frown, sizing us up. He put his hand on the Chevelle's fender and wore wonderment over his expression. I thought either he really dug primo classic cars, or he was dense in the head.

"Do you know where the wedding is?" asked Jenny.

The question perked the astonished mind, and he nodded.

"Is it far?" asked Jenny. I could tell by her tone she considered him sub-curve as well.

He pointed.

"Where? How far?" Jenny asked as she got out of the car.

The child in the rough attire started walking, presumably expecting us to follow. I didn't like leaving the car like that, but I didn't have much choice. I dropped the keys into my pocket and followed Jenny, who followed the boy.

Jenny wore flat woven hemp slip-ons, and I wore brown loafers. Uncomfortable, but there isn't much walking involved in a wedding. I should've been fine, but after five minutes up the dusty road, my feet ached. The child led the way along the hard-packed gravel road and up to a dirt laneway.

Ahead there were three old trucks, like really old, and I calculated how much money the owners had probably wasted keeping them in decent shape. The closer we got, the more that number dropped. The trucks had chipped paint, dented fenders and rusty spots, but they felt as if it was wear and not age. I thought maybe someone had salvaged them for sale, or hadn't yet started the restoration. Either way it seemed strange for them to be parked out in the sun like they were, value paling under the pounding rays.

"Do you smell that?" Jenny asked.

This was the scent of an active farm. There were a dozen or so horses hitched outside the barn, so maybe this was the case.

The kid pointed at the barn door and then ran away.

"This doesn't look right," said Jenny.

"Maybe they have a phone." I'd just put my cell back into my pocket. There wasn't a hint of signal finding me. It made me feel naked on top of everything else.

I opened the door slowly and heard a voice. There was a wedding underway. I turned back to Jenny and put my finger to my lips, signaling that she leave her complaints outside the door. I couldn't see the bride or the groom, but the room was almost barren. I counted twenty-one people, two groups of nine besides the main event. All sat, some waved fans in front of their faces, but it appeared like most other weddings, only drabber.

The barn was a part of a working farm for sure, and I wondered why the people had bothered. They could marry in a church or a field a hell of a lot easier than pushing aside all the hay and straw.

"This isn't the right wedding," Jenny whispered.

"Do you, Abner Moon, take this woman to be your wife?" the preacher man asked.

I felt ugly about encroaching on a couple's *special day*.

"Let's wait outside," I whispered and Jenny opened the plank-wood door open far enough to step outside. The sun blasted into our eyes. The change from dim to bright isn't as easy as the opposite, and we stood a moment, letting our sights adjust before moving along.

"Leavin' early?" asked a harsh voice. There was a laugh in the man's throat behind the words, like an un-hawked phlegm wad.

Still blinking away sunspots, I stared down the barrel of a shotgun.

"They ain't goin' nowhere, is yas?" asked a second man. He had two grey revolvers.

Jenny latched onto my arm like a leech to a swimmer, like she wasn't banging some college-aged stud. There were four men outside the barn, not including myself. All wore billowy button-up shirts, loose slacks, worn black boots, and straw hats. Firearms at the ready.

"We's all attendin' this shindig," said the man with the revolvers. He wore a grin, showing a line of slimy, yellowed teeth.

The men all stank of sweat, and filth, and liquor.

I backed a step. Jenny wasn't moving, so I nudged her with my elbow. We stepped through the door. The bride and groom were on their way toward us. Big smiles to go 'round.

"That's my girl, Abna'," said the grinning man. He lifted his arm only inches from my cheek and pulled the trigger. The report toppled me, sending a hollow ping through the center of everything I heard.

Screaming ensued. The cows joined from below like ill-tuned backup singers.

"Oh, Jesus, Jesus!" said the bride, cradling the groom's caved head in her arms.

The foursome rounded up the group--Jenny and myself included--in the group. The preacher took it upon himself to go on the high and mighty offensive, offering a spot in Hell to each of the men.

"Since that's all figured, I reckon I gots nothin' ta

lose," said the grinning man. He levelled the barrel of his revolver and pulled the trigger, muzzle against the preacher's forehead. The weapon exploded in the man's hand. Shrapnel tore off in every direction. The preacher fell into a heap, his soul on its journey from the flesh. The shooter's hand was destroyed as if by result of sinning.

My life flashed, in a manner. I'd wasted so much time. The future flashed. There was a bullet-ridden image of myself lying still in the dust and straw, half of my face gone from a shotgun blast, and I wanted to cry out and tear away from that place screaming that somebody broke the rules and that the world didn't work this way.

"Sonofabitch, you see, you see what happens!" the man with the ruined hand yelled as if the wedding crowd was to blame for the misfire.

A woman, Abner's mother to guess based on the look in her eyes, lashed out at the grinning man. "Ged off'm!"

The first man we encountered lifted his shotgun and pulled the trigger. Abner's mother took much of it, but the grinning man lost what little grin he had left after the shot found a home in both. A two for one deal!

"Shot me, you pig," he howled, crawling backwards as if he might back out of the pain.

Pandemonium ensued, and shots rang out in every direction. A rifle fell into the hands of the wedding guests, and the gunners toppled as fast as the wedding guests. Everything unraveled in a matter of about a dozen seconds.

Jenny had me by the arm, and she pointed toward the door. The bride was crawling and making good time. There was some cover thanks to the square bale benches. I pushed Jenny forward, and we chased after the bride.

From outside, we heard more shots from within the barn, until they stopped. Not a body moaned or screamed. The man from the back stepped out, his shirt was red polka dots, and he looked around wildly. He saw us. His eyes were heavy and nasty. We broke for a field, following the bride.

Jenny was never much of a track star. The bride was in a long dress. My loafers shot pain up through my legs. A trifecta of bad stuff. Bullets zoomed and hissed near our heads. Dirt struck my hand from a ricochet, and for a second, I thought I was dead. I recovered, and thanks to my body knowing better than my panic, my legs kept moving and my heart still pumped. The man gained on us. He gave up on his shooting for the time. He focused instead on the chase, gaining, getting closer and closer with every quick-patter heartbeat.

"What do you want?" I screamed as if I might talk him out of it.

"Goin' ta die!" he called back at me.

"Why?" I yelled over my shoulder.

I was sure I could feel his breath.

I thought maybe I could talk him out of killing us. Sales was my business, after all. This was stupid. Putting a man behind the wheel isn't the same negotiation as talking a man out of murder, especially when he's on a roll.

"Ever'body dies," he said.

The bride tripped over her dress.

Jenny fell over the bride.

I had plenty of time to sidestep.

All at once, my mind ran through the horrid things Jenny had done and had said. I envisioned an off-the-blocks burst of energy that put feet and then metres between the man and me. Instead, I knelt beside my wife, knowing I would die. I'd loved her deeply, once upon a time.

The man was right there. He loaded his shooter as he gasped for air. "Ya shouldn'a... done'at... shouldn'a left...poor Honus," said the man. His attention, at least for the time being, was on the bride.

"One date!" she cried.

Boom!

The bride coughed and fell back into the grass on the edge of the field. The hole in her chest silenced the excitement. The barrel shifted toward Jenny.

"You's all the same," said the man.

Luck fell momentarily as he squeezed the trigger, and it let out only a dull tick. Jenny saw her chance and kicked him in the ankle as he fiddled with the dud round.

"Shitters!" he shouted and squeezed after the junk round fell.

I leapt to my feet. The air whizzed over my shoulder as I pounced on him. We rolled and wrestled, and he let go two more shots, hitting nothing of consequence.

"Gon' die!" he squeezed again and missed.

Jenny moaned. Stupidly, I released myself from the gunner's one-hand grip and skittered to Jenny. Blood bubbled from her shoulder.

"Y'all both die now."

I turned, holding Jenny in my arms, and tried my salesman's grin. The man shook his head and aimed. I went blank. I didn't consider running or fighting. I slumped, a deer staring down a set of lights from a Mack truck, stupid vacant grin on my face.

I heard the shot, or at least I think I heard the shot. It wasn't over.

There was music and cheers.

I opened my eyes and looked around.

It was a wedding.

There were hundreds of people standing under tents in the field next to ours. Relief washed over me, and I jumped to my feet. A thick layer of dust covered my blue pants. I brushed while I walked. I cast a glance backwards. Jenny held her bloodied shoulder.

"What... goddamn what...?" she mumbled.

"I know what you did," I blurted. "You can call your boyfriend for a ride home."

Her mouth opened and closed soundlessly. I started out for the road. Nobody noticed me leave, and Jenny didn't try to stop me.

My phone had bars, and I called for a tow. I got back to the car long before the tow arrived. I questioned the reality of what had happened and denied it the entire walk. I knew there was no way what I saw happen had happened.

The driver pulled up, and he held a filthy arm out the window, a classic revolver pointed at me. He grinned. "Dyin' time, boy!" he shouted, and I fell back.

"Ya all right? Got a flat, yeah?" asked the driver. A soft man wearing an Indians hat and blue coveralls. No old-timey shooter.

I explained my flat and that I was at a wedding.

"Better that you're not driving. Got some wine on ya." The driver grinned at me as if looking at man in the bag. He hooked the Chevelle. "This is some cherry whip. Yours?"

There were blood and strands of straw on my shirt. There was dirt on my knees. I nodded.

As we rode, he explained the story of the Moon wedding murders nearly fifty years earlier, to the day, he thought, just maybe. I gawked vacantly at the passing shoulder, not hearing the man, lost in the reverie of possibility and impossibility.

~/~

At home, I packed Jenny's things. She wouldn't argue. I'd sent a ten-second .avi to her email with the subject line More available upon request. She wasn't stupid. She'd see how things were apt to go.

And she did.

Sometimes I dream about it all. That shooter hides in my closet, under my bed, in the backseat of my Chevelle, but he never finishes the job. I wake and try to connect the dots, but they don't make sense. I don't know how I got there, and I don't know how I got away, but I know I'll never go down that road again.

One marriage was enough for me.

Sheep's Clothing

Dale Hollin

"I've been waiting for you."

She glanced to the window. Her reflection seemed pale and distraught compared to his. She watched as the image altered and focused upon her being impaled by him; her lip bleeding from the orgasmic pleasure of her own teeth biting into it. She thought of the wolf. Her reflection always showed the scars of the wolf. She pictured the mannequins, protected safely beyond the glass, with shattered holes in their throats and bare arms reaching for god in the fluorescent light.

Gloria turned from the mannequins and smiled, biting her tongue. They never moved. Behind the glass, they would always remain what they were. Dead. As much as the doll may attempt to bleed, it never will. She raised her eyes and gazed at the shade of the moon upon the glass. A full moon brighter than the city. She lowered her head, waiting for the voice.

Have you ever fucked a ghost?

She smiled and felt her teeth with her tongue. The dolls behind the window became dim; their small plastic breasts pushing forward, only to enhance the false light from the ceiling panels. His hand touched her shoulder. The touch of the wolf always felt warmer in the moonlight.

"See something you like, my love?"

His reflection was dark and cold. She lifted her hand slowly and held it suspended in front of her. In the glass, the blush on his face held no heat. He looked less vibrant. If she could only know his reflection, he wouldn't be able to control her so. She closed her eyes and smiled as he lowered his hand and touched the silver pentacle hanging from a chain between her breasts.

"I do love the taste of silver on my tongue, especially when covered with your sweat. Would you like I buy you the outfit in the window? Or would you rather I remove the one you're wearing? I suppose we could do both, but the store will still be here tomorrow. I'm not so sure about us."

He peered beneath the neckline of her blouse, watching her breath and heartbeat become more rapid. His face lowered closer to her lips, and he inhaled the scent of her words as she spoke.

"I want nothing worn by these lifeless models. Where will you take me?"

She felt him glance over her shoulder and bare his teeth in a grin. A younger man was standing in the near distance, watching them. There were always men watching her when the two of them were out. She thought the wolf seemed to enjoy it. It sometimes made her afraid that he did. His face became warmer, and she glanced back at the man. The wolf lifted his head, and the younger man lowered his, glancing to his watch before turning away from them.

"There's something I have to do. Go to a room. I'll find you."

She opened her eyes and stared into the glass. He was gone. Gloria inhaled through her nose and could no longer feel his scent. What was his name? She remembered having it engraved what seemed like long ago. The letters seemed jumbled in her mind. She touched the shop window's glass, tracing random consonants on the pane with her fingertip. The dolls posing before her became sheened in a dark mist, gasping orgasmic breaths and whispers.

She turned and left the mannequins to their fate. She could feel the empty gazes penetrating her back. The city lights seemed to dim. The dolls had no scent to follow her, only silent voices which struggled to escape the holes which he had torn in their plastic throats. She listened closely for them, but could only hear her footsteps clamoring upon the cement, leading her to the row of motels set in bright neon lighting a few blocks away. The wolf was always within these lights. She would catch his scent again, comfortably, before reaching them.

A cloud passed in front of the moon, and she felt the younger man walking in the distance behind her. She glanced over her shoulder quickly, but didn't see him. The city wasn't quite dead yet, and a sparse crowd left her unable to choose his form from the shadows of the others. She knew he was there, though. Even beyond her sense of smell, she knew.

The bright red light of the motel sign grinned down at her and she exhaled. The younger one moved closer. Gloria opened the door and walked into the small, single room lobby to the empty desk counter. The scent of both the wolf and the younger one were clean now. They were both in the lot, lurking. A door opened.

"You need something, ma'am?"

The clerk stepped forward, smelling of semen and cheap cologne. His light hair was matted to his forehead with a sweat not his own. She looked over her shoulder and felt a solitary shadow crossing the lot. She turned back to the clerk.

"I just need a room for the night."

He spun the clipboard to face her and glanced to the clock. It was 11:03.

"Just sign here. Do you have an ID, miss?"

She engraved a name upon the white tablet with the pen. The blue ink looked dry and transparent.

"No. I seem to have misplaced it."

His snort was like a serpent's hiss as he pulled the clipboard away, placing it under the counter.

"Yeah. So many people who open that door have a funny habit of losing their IDs. It's gonna be twenty dollars more without it. For deposit reasons. Non-refundable, you understand."

She handed him the money and glanced to the clock. He handed her a key, and she bared her teeth, turning from the desk and opening the door. The night wind ran dark fingers through her hair, and her face became warm as she walked towards the room. The younger man was near. The scent of the wolf overpowered his, and she closed her eyes, placing the palm of her left hand on her door while lowering the key. The breath felt hot on the back of her neck, and she smiled. She opened the door and stood silent, staring into the darkness of the rented chamber.

"Hi. I followed you here. You looked lonely. I hope you don't mind. My name's David."

She passed through the entrance and flipped on the lamp through the switch beside the doorway. He watched her turn back to him, her lips upturned slightly.

"Yes. I had a feeling you'd show up, David. You may come in, if you like. I may not always make the best company, but I don't think I'd mind yours now."

The scent of the wolf was faint, but near. She smelled this "David" more purely. He removed his jacket and lifted a container from an inside pocket.

"I have some gin, if you'd like a drink."

She bared her teeth and walked slowly to the sink and counter at the back of the room. The small plastic cups were sealed in cellophane. She glanced in the mirror and watched his reflection move closer.

"Gin will be fine."

He took the cups from her, removing the packaging and filled each to the point of being half empty. She lifted one of them from his hand and stared into his face as she drank. He was quite attractive, she thought. His head turned back towards the television set. She knew it was a sign of nervousness.

"Go ahead and find something on the set, if you want. Make yourself comfortable." She handed him the empty cup. "I'm gonna freshen up a bit."

He watched her walk into the bathroom and close the door. A shadow crossed the reflection above the sink as he set the cups on the counter and refilled them. Maybe he would turn the television on. The silence in the room rang as a constant and high pitch in his ears. He walked over to the set and turned it on with the remote placed black and stagnant atop it. The warbling voices of past ghosts began droning before the screen lit. He sat on the edge of the bed and heard the door of the bathroom open.

"Did you find something on?"

She walked into the room unclothed. His eyes roamed, starting at her bare feet and moving upward over her body. Another shadow passed quickly across the mirror beside her. He stared at her pallid throat and noticed a deep scratch where her neck met her collarbone. She was beautiful.

"You haven't told me your name."

She bared her teeth and moved towards him, standing still between him and the lit screen. He watched the shimmering light of the black and white film dance chaotically upon the skin of her inner thighs.

"You already know my name. You know that."

He leaned back onto the bed. The scent of the wolf became stronger every time she inhaled. She leaned forward and pulled open the front of his pants, feeling the lukewarm and metallic zipper surrender and fall as she lowered her hand. His breathing became more strained, and she glanced towards the mirror set above the sink, which held the empty light from the TV casting grey and jagged dancers upon the drawn curtains across the room.

She yanked down hard on the divided seam of his slacks and exposed him. His breath quickened, and she grasped him fully in her hand. He seemed larger than he was within her fingers and knew it was the heat of the wolf within his flesh that made it seem so. She lowered her face and tasted the salt and sting of him burning, cast sweetly upon her tongue and back of her throat.

Her fist removed him from her lips, and she

stood, staring down at him as he glanced towards the mirror. He looked back into her face and exhaled, pushing himself back fully across the bed. He looked towards the door and then back at her teeth.

"Would you like to lie down with me?"

Her nostrils flared, and she raked her fingers through her hair, before lowering her hand and clenching her nipple. He watched it turn darker and swollen. She climbed forward onto the mattress, lifting his shirt from his chest and holding it under his chin.

"I really don't feel like lying down with anyone. You're not all the way undressed yet. Don't you want your clothes on the floor?"

He pulled his shirt over his head and flung it aside. The film droning behind her back illuminated her hips with a dim flickering light as she straddled him and impaled herself. He rolled his eyes into his head and exhaled, staring at the barren wall which blocked his view of the reflection. Her face moved closer to his and then threw her head back. The scent of pine and musk made him gasp harder as he watched her form rise and descend more frantically. His eyes followed her breasts as they shifted violently in their course from heaven to hell, the sweat between them collecting on her fingers as she moved them rhythmically up and down.

She placed the wet fingertips in her mouth and bared her teeth as she felt his body convulse beneath her. His mouth became a dark oval vacuum, unable to intake fully the smell of the air in before it. She lifted herself and fell rabidly in quick, repetitive jerks until she felt him begin to dissolve within her. He moaned and covered his face with his hands.

"Can you speak my name yet now that I've drowned you?"

She moved from atop him, swinging her legs over the edge of the mattress near the bedside end table. His form rolled slowly over on its side, facing the wall which absorbed his deep breaths and echoed them back to her. She listened and became calmer each time he exhaled. He wasn't going to speak her name. He was going to lie still and silent.

She stood and walked to the curtain, pulling it back. The night masked the light of the moon and neon sign in front of the motel. The wolf stood still in front of her door, baring his teeth. She opened the lock and looked down at the blade gripped tightly in her hand. *He should have spoken my name.* She let the curtain fall and walked back to the bed, staring down at the one who had come uninvited. The barely visible purple line on the side of his neck began to bulge, as if wanting release from the bondage of the skin. She lifted the blade and opened him. The form immediately pulled forward and raised his hand in an attempt to stifle the liberty of the draught. He began gasping as he did before while impaling her. She bared her teeth and loved him. The blood from his throat fell and intermingled with their sweat on the mattress, making love in a union of color and scent. She watched his face grow pale and relaxed and smiled when he slept.

A shadow crept into the reflection across the room. She glanced up and walked over to the sink, twisting the tap. The water carried the music of a cascade, and she cupped the draught in her hands, lifting it to her face and closing her eyes. She inhaled through her nose and smelled the familiar scent. Her back became warm, and she lifted herself.

"Did you like who I became tonight?"

She felt the wound on her collarbone become hot, and she opened her eyes. His hand moved slowly from her neck and downward between her breasts. She stared at him in the glass and lowered her fingers to her abdomen. The warmth within her became brighter, and his reflection dimmed to a pale shadow.

"The one you brought here tonight was very nice. I think he served his purpose well. You know I'll always love you."

The wolf lowered his eyes and felt himself pale. She smiled and closed her eyes. The fingers touching herself becoming wet. The sound of the water became as music and she tilted her head to its gentle lullaby. She lifted the hand from her skin and felt part of herself swim within her. The scent of the wolf was gone.

She walked over to the bed and laid beside the corpse, caressing the heat within her belly. The scent of the wolf was now within her. She knew her spell controlled him now. She bared her teeth.

The Heritage Drug Project

Hugh A.D. Spencer

Brown's Line and Horner Avenue

Fuller was down to three pills. That wasn't going to get him to lunch, let alone through the rest of the day. He could already feel his asshole starting to burn and spasm.

Fuller rolled his ancient Austin into the parking lot of the Save-A-Lot Family Drug Mart. The shop had been there for years, originally an Independent Druggist Association outlet, now part of the Rexall chain. Changes like this always had pluses and minuses.

He shut off the ignition, and the garbled screech of the car's emergency brake sounded like he'd just strangled a pterosaur. Appropriate, the Austin probably came off the assembly line some time during the early Cretaceous. Fuller slammed the car door shut (only way to close it properly) and walked over to the store entrance.

The plus side of Save-A-Lot being a part of a big chain was that their drugs tended to be of a slightly higher quality, which meant they weren't so likely to burn out the lining of your stomach when you took five to ten times the recommended dose several times a day. The cheaper stuff could get a bit nasty.

The minus side was that the bigger chains were usually required to keep more detailed records of their transactions. Which meant that the pharmacists tended to be more observant of who was buying what and how often. Which, in turn, meant Fuller had to make strategic adjustments to his visitation schedule.

In other words, he couldn't be seen there too often.

Fuller pushed on the door handle. The door stayed shut.

The sudden rush of panic sent a sharp and painful leak of fluid into his underpants. Not a big leak, not likely to smell too bad, but a reminder that he was starting to lose control of his bodily functions.

What the hell was going on here? They didn't change the opening to noon, did they? Some of the stores were starting to do that to save on staff costs. Fuller checked the sign on the door. No, it still said they opened at 8:00 A.M. He had arranged to arrive fashionably, and unsuspiciously, late-ish at 9:30.

Fuller pushed on the handle again, this time a little harder. The door shuddered a bit and popped open. Guess it must have been just a little stuck from the cold.

It was rarely a good idea to rush directly to the pharmacist's counter. Fuller made sure he spent some time looking at the batteries and SD cards over at the photography section. Next, he checked out the ribbed condoms and "stimulating gels" at family planning aisle (purely theoretical interest there) before sidling up to his objective. Even there, he feigned an interest in vitamins for a minute or two. There was a sale in vitamins B and D, so he decided to complete his disguise by picking up a bottle of each.

Harry was the pharmacist on duty. Fuller didn't need the name tag to know that. He knew Harry well. Harry was a nice guy, always cheerful, always trying to be helpful. Fuller's theory was that Harry really wanted to be a doctor but had to settle for being a druggist in his calling to combat human suffering. Not that Fuller was criticizing the guy. He really needed Harry this morning.

"Good morning." Fuller put on his pained and just a little pathetic smile. It was a smile he hoped resembled that of a nice, respectable person who just happened to be having some kind of medical problem through no fault of his own.

"Good morrow to you!" Harry responded with a smile that was a lot less calculated than Fuller's. "What can I do you for this fine day?"

Fuller hoped there wasn't any recognition in Harry's smile. "Do you have any..." Fuller paused as if he wasn't quite sure of the correct name. "...acetaminophen? With codeine?"

"Why sure!" Harry was still smiling, which at this point Fuller took to be a very good sign. "Do you want name brand or generic?"

"Is the generic less expensive?" Fuller hoped this question sounded really naïve.

"Considerably." Harry opened the drawer containing the necessary substances. "What size would you like? fifty tablets, thirty, or a hundred?"

"Do you have anything larger?" Fuller immediately realized he was probably pushing things at this point.

For the first time, Harry seemed a little hesitant.

"It does come in bottles of two hundred, but that's an awful lot of medication to have without a prescription."

Fuller knew he would have to play the rest of this transaction just right. He put the two bottles of vitamins on the counter. Promise of a sure sale was always very persuasive. "I know, it's just that I'm going abroad, and I don't know what help I'll be able to get there."

Harry nodded, and his big smile came back. "Just don't try cross the US border with this stuff. They'll nail your ass."

Outside, Fuller threw his bag of pills onto the passenger seat and climbed into the Austin. He felt like the shit that was threatening to explode into his pants.

Not an uncommon feeling for him.

Bathurst Street and Wilson Avenue

Home. Such as it was, thought Fuller. As a bedsit in the basement of an old house, it was more like a bomb crater with a concrete floor, a hot plate and a TV set. The TV was a cathode ray job, none of that new-fangled flat-screen nonsense.

Without removing his coat, Fuller filled a plastic tumbler with some brown tap water, twisted the cap of the bottle and shook eight pills into his hand. Although he'd trained his throat to swallow all eight at once, he tried to convince himself he wasn't completely desperate at this point, and so he downed them in two lots of four with large gulps of water to make it a more comfortable experience.

Chemical obligations met, Fuller took off his coat, lay down on the coach, and turned on the TV.

It was some nostalgia show: a documentary about The Prisoner series. Fuller wished they'd rerun that show. Nowadays all he ever seemed to get was The Simpsons and Family Guy.

Eventually, the familiar good slow glow started. It began by easing the pain around his rectum, up through his stomach to the base of his brain and finally relaxing his mouth into the first real smile of the day. Then it spread into his eyes, which made him feel happy and even made the inside of his dark grimy bedsit look pretty good. The only problem was that he had to take a little bit more codeine to get that glow going. That and the fact that the drug made his penis shrivel and go numb.

Then there was another kind of glow. It came from under the bathroom door.

"Shit." Fuller was about to get a visit from Mr. Bruce, A.K.A. Professor Killjoy. Of course,

Mr. Bruce was going to want his samples.

Yonge Street and Yorkdale Avenue

Even though it was a lot of paper to hump around on the subway, Fuller wanted to work at the Main Reference Library, and that was the price he had to pay. Besides, sometimes it was good to get the hell out of the apartment. It kept him from adding extra doses to his regimen.

Fuller had rules. Four doses a day: 08:00, 12:00, 17:00, and 23:00. Eight tablets per dose. Sometimes ten on bad days. On good days that added up to 256 grains of codeine. God knows how much caffeine and acetaminophen and other crap was getting pumped into his bloodstream in the process.

It didn't matter. What really counted was getting

those opiates where they needed to go. Mr. Bruce and his body told him that on a very regular basis. But goddamn it, no matter how much he wanted to, how much Mr. Bruce wanted him to, he was not, was not going to cross the eight (well, sometimes ten) tablets line. To be fair, Mr. Bruce never came out and told him to up his doses. That seemed to go against the strange man's code of ethics. Mr. Bruce would just sometimes ask if Fuller needed to borrow some cash to buy his drugs.

"And remember…" Mr. Bruce would sometimes say when he'd pack up the samples and head for the glowing door. "…you were like this when we found you."

Thank you for reminding me this is all my fault, Fuller would think.

So, for whatever reason, being in the Reference Library seemed to keep that resolution on days when he was feeling even weaker than usual.

Fuller walked into the main lobby and gazed at all the attractive young people working away at their sleek, beautiful computers. What were those things called? Lab tops? Nedbooks? Ibods? Some days, Fuller wondered if he ought to get one of those things and find out what all this personal computing and internet stuff was all about. There were probably a few secondhand ones around that he could afford.

He would think, he would dream, but that was all just inner crazy talk. Fuller knew there was no way that he could handle that big a change in his life.

He found his usual cubicle and spread his papers over the simulated wood surface. Soviet scientific documents from 1960-1980. Recently declassified. Five dollars a page.

Fortunately, Soviet scientists were pretty verbose people. Maybe nobody listened to them in their daily lives, and they needed to express themselves. But even with all those pages there never seemed to be enough money. He needed the cash from Mr. Bruce's visits to get him through the month. Fuller wished he was better at budgeting, but he hadn't been able to figure out his bank statements in over fifteen years.

At least the latest bunch of papers was pretty interesting. Series of publications from a radio astronomer at the University of Omsk who was collaborating with some un-named remote sensing specialists.

"...radio waves are too primitive, too obvious a means of communicating between the stars..."

Fuller stopped and studied the words that had just flowed out of his fountain pen. The original Russian was much more eloquent, almost poetic. Fuller did the best that he could with the translation.

Bathurst Street and Wilson Avenue

In spite of Fuller's efforts to persuade him otherwise, Mr. Bruce insisted on inserting the needles in his sphincter.

"What about my temple? Or up my nose?" Those entry points were just as painful, but they weren't as embarrassing.

"Sorry, buddy." Mr. Bruce put on his fake-sympathy face. "We seem to get the best samples from your butt."

All Fuller could do in situations like that were to grab onto the bed sheets or the couch cushions and try not to whimper too loudly. Mr. Bruce was cool with the whole procedure. He just leaned back into

Fuller's most comfortable (and only) chair and drank some of Fuller's brown tap water. "Do you know what my job was before I got recruited by the Superculture?"

"Ah..." At that moment Fuller wondered why an infinite number of infinitely advanced extraterrestrial civilizations couldn't have given Mr. Bruce something as simple as a local anesthetic. "You haven't mentioned it."

Fuller was dimly pleased that he'd been able to speak those words without crying.

"I used to work for the Ministry of Agriculture." Mr. Bruce smiled a little, sad smile. With what, nostalgia? "I used to cultivate heritage crops."

"What are--ugh!" The pulse in Fuller's rectum was right next to the needle, so every once in a while, he'd get bolts of white-hot pain shooting up his spine. "Heritage crops?"

"Seeds that nobody plants anymore." Mr. Bruce got up and poured himself another glass of brown water. "But that we don't want to go extinct."

"Sounds like very relaxing work." And almost as lonely as my job, thought Fuller.

"It's pretty important." Mr. Bruce sighed and sat back down. "And was an excellent qualification for my current assignment."

Fuller wondered about that as Mr. Bruce sucked back half the glass of water.

"That wasn't very good at all," Mr. Bruce pronounced as he set the glass on the arm of the chair. "Why don't you ever have any booze around here?"

"I can only handle one substance abuse problem at a time."

Bay and Bloor Streets

The PharmaSave at the Manulife Centre required a completely different approach. Years back, Fuller found the place to be a really easy hit. It was dead center in the City's business district, which meant hundreds of people were pouring through there every lunch hour. All of them were in a hurry and without the patience to deal with other people's bullshit. The pharmacists shared the same attitudes as their customers.

For months and months, Fuller was able to go there and score as much codeine as he wanted, and nobody asked any questions. People were just too busy to care. It didn't last, though. For someone to work in this environment they had to be pretty smart and extremely alert – just like Fuller. One day Fuller's "detecto-sense" went off. He had a feeling the young lady pharmacist with the $1800 glasses was contemplating asking him a few questions about the second bottle of two hundred tablets of Tylenol #1 he'd purchased from her in three weeks.

Time to enter disguise-mode. Nothing too complicated; fake beards and false noses were complicated and ultimately ineffective. A much subtler methodology was needed.

Fuller hunched up his back, as if in considerable pain and whispered: "Excuse me."

The affluent pharmacist looked at him through those very expensive glasses. "Can I help you?"

"I, uh, hope so." Fuller tapped his cheek. "I just got a root canal."

A flicker of sympathy was evident--even from behind those giant lenses. Maybe she'd had a few root canals herself.

"I think my dentist was supposed to give me a prescription for the pain."

"That's usually what happens."

"But there were a lot of other patients there." Fuller slurred his words just a tiny bit as if he was still talking through the remaining of effects of the freezing. "I think he forgot about me."

"Oh, dear."

Sympathy. He had her now. Fuller was careful not to smile. "Can you suggest anything?"

The pharmacist pulled out a large white bottle. "This has eight grains of codeine and two tablets three times a day should get you through the pain."

"Isn't this kind of a lot?" Jackpot. Two hundred tablets.

The pharmacist smiled. "It's lot cheaper if you buy the generic brand and get the largest size possible."

Fuller had definitely hit all the right buttons. He felt a complex mix of triumph and shame. "Thank you so much."

Bathurst Street and Wilson Avenue

And home again.

This time Mr. Bruce decided to be nice and extract the blood through one of Fuller's nipples. Painful, but it could have been much worse.

"Heritage crops are very important." Fuller wondered why Mr. Bruce was being so expansive these days. "What would happen if some disease, some pandemic, wiped out all the grains we were growing today?"

"I don't know." Frankly unless the disease wiped out the opium crop, Fuller didn't care that much.

"Our food supply would run out in less than eight months."

"That's not good." Yeah, even though he was an addict, Fuller did have to eat every once in a while. "I guess we'd starve."

"Not if we maintain our heritage crops." Mr. Bruce looked very pleased with himself. "These antique grains might not be as tasty or as fertile as some of the new genetically modified strains..." At this point, Mr. Bruce started manipulating Fuller's penis. Tonight, it seemed to be necessary to collect a sperm sample; Fuller felt things had been going too well up until then. "...but they will get us through the blight."

This was not going to be a pleasant experience. Fuller did not find Mr. Bruce particularly attractive, and the situation wasn't particularly sexy. The best thing for Fuller to do was to think about work.

The day's pile had more translations from that Soviet Astronomer. The guy kept going on about the ineffectiveness of radio waves as a media of communication between interstellar civilizations:

"...because sentience, self-awareness and creativity are ultimately indefinable..." Fuller was sure he wasn't doing justice to the original Russian "...we should explore the natural quantum processes of cognition as the basis for instant information exchange between star systems."

Fuller found that kind of talk much sexier than anything that Mr. Bruce might be doing. Eventually Mr. Bruce gave up on the masturbatory process and stuck a needle up Fuller's urethra. Then he collected up the various vials of fluid and got ready to walk through the wall.

"Try not to get too discouraged, Mr. Fuller." Mr.

Bruce stepped into the glow. "You're making an important contribution."

Bathurst Street and Wilson Avenue (Again)

The telephone rang. This happened so rarely Fuller had been thinking about getting the thing disconnected.

"Hello?" Fuller had to answer. He was probably the owner of the last rotary phone in the northern hemisphere. This was fun for historical reasons, but it meant services like call display and voice messaging were completely impossible.

"Is this Stephen Fuller?" A woman's voice asked the question. Fuller kind of remembered what women sounded like.

"Yes." He wondered if this was a good thing to admit to someone he couldn't see. However, he couldn't think of a good reason not to tell the truth.

"Stephen." There was something slightly familiar about the voice now. "It's Jean."

"Jean?" Something at the back of Fuller's mind told him that he was being incredibly thick.

"Jean Bilious from Lakeshore Collegiate."

Jean?!

"Do you remember me?"

It felt like Fuller hit the floor. Except that it didn't hurt so much. Indeed he did remember her.

Queen Street West and John Street

This was one of the hippest drug stores in the city. Lots of bottles of "herbal" remedies and "alternative" medications. Tricky place to take down. "Back pain" was probably the best tactic.

"Have you considered seeing a chiropractor?"

The pharmacist was new, so at least there was no recognition factor.

"Yes." Fuller sighed and blinked, as if he was fighting off some kind of spasm. "I think it was a bad adjustment that got me into this situation."

Fuller did not like the fact that Howard (the name on the tag) was wearing glasses with heavy black frames. It was like the man was wearing a mask. Very hard to read to read his expressions.

"That's pretty unusual." Howard the Pharmacist's tone suggested that he did not appreciate criticisms of fellow health care professionals. "Maybe you should try therapeutic massage."

Fuller was going to have to come on strong. Really, he should have come in with another infected root canal. Nobody likes dentists.

"That's a good suggestion." Fuller put his hands on the counter and leaned forward as if he was trying to ease the pressure off his back. "But in the meantime, I need something to keep me going until I can make an appointment."

Howard folded his arms. "What did you have in mind?"

Just give me the goddamned opiates! Was what Fuller wanted to scream. Instead he used very nicest indoor voice. "Do you have any aspirin with codeine?"

Howard didn't say anything as he opened a drawer and put a small white bottle on the counter. thirty caplets. The smallest amount available.

"Do you have anything larger? I don't want to come back here right away."

Howard shook his head. "That's all I have."

"I don't mind paying extra for a brand name."

God, Fuller knew how pathetic he sounded.

"That's the only size we carry."

Fuller knew that it was not a good idea to push this one any further. Thirty fucking caplets! That wouldn't get him through lunch tomorrow.

When he walked out of the drug store, Fuller started making calculations. If he got on the subway right away, he might be able to get to Yorkdale Mall and check out that new Shopper's Drug Mart, and still get home in time to make his deadline.

Jean.

He realized Plan B was not going to work. Fuller had agreed to meet her for dinner.

Dundas Street West and Beatrice Road

"So, it's remote sensing and stuff like that?"

Jean was eating the smallest sandwich possible without the use of nanotechnology. With a skinny person, such a meal would have been intolerable, but Jean was not like that, and Fuller sensed she was pretty comfortable with her body. Fuller remembered why he loved her so much way back when.

"That kind of thing shows up every once in a while." Fuller used a plastic fork to pierce a slab of orange cabbage. "But mostly it's papers on how to fuel cars with potato extract or how to cure the common cold by pouring molasses up your nose."

"Sounds fun." Jean picked up a piece of his orange cabbage and tucked it into her mouth. Fuller liked that she stole food off his plate. Somehow Jean understood that the best kimchi in Canada was sold in this tiny boho cafe just off the alternate theatre district.

"I wish more of it was."

"Was what?"

"Fun."

Fuller couldn't believe how good Jean looked. She'd started to cultivate a sense of style early on in high school, and she'd just kept on going.

"Most of it is pretty boring," Fuller continued. "But it pays the bills."

"I guess that's too bad." Jean started in on her third glass of red wine. "Don't worry, I'm taking a taxi home."

So decadent. So responsible. So Jean.

"No." Fuller swallowed the last of his spiced cabbage. "It's just about the level of complexity that I can handle."

Jean looked at him with an expression that was a little...sad? "So that's really all you do? Translations?"

"The agency says they have enough in their archives to keep me going until I'm ninety-five." Fuller wasn't sure if he should be proud or embarrassed.

Jean frowned a little and took another sip of red.

"Is there something wrong with that?" Fuller thought that she would have been happy for him.

"I guess job security is a good thing..."

"Yes, it is."

Jean put her glass down. "It just seems a little...private."

"Private?" Fuller glanced at his glass. Red wine was an ambivalent thing for him. "Is that a bad thing?"

"No, no." Jean turned and looked out the window at whatever might be happening out there. "I just always thought that...you'd end up doing something more out there."

Out there? What the hell was that supposed to mean?

Jean put her hand on his. "Privacy was what made it so hard to find you."

"Sorry about that." Fuller drank some of his wine and tried not be annoyed. Being 'out there' wasn't easy when you had to spend at least fifty percent of your waking hours feeding your habit, however semi-legal it might be.

"No need to apologize." Jean knocked back half of her glass. "It's just that you're not on Facebook or Instagram or even Blogspot, as far as I can tell."

"What's Facebook?"

Jean blinked. "You've never heard of Facebook?"

Fuller shook his head.

"What about Twitter?"

Fuller shrugged. "Isn't that what birds do?"

"Stephen, this is like that old TV show, Buck Rogers." Fuller was surprised by her expression. Pity? "Have you been in suspended animation for the last thirty-five years?"

She didn't just touch his hand this time. She gave it a hard squeeze. Even though all the residual codeine in his bloodstream made most of his body (especially the parts between his legs) pretty numb most of the time...Jean's strong contact made him feel good. Really, really good.

"I don't know about that." Yes, suspended animation, suspended life was exactly how it had been since he'd started seriously using. "But I've never owned a computer."

Jean's eyes went very wide and it looked like she might fall out of her chair. "What?! I mean...how?"

Once again Fuller shrugged. "Never saw the

need for one." And he was worried that he'd just get into more trouble if he had one.

"How can you even function?" Jean shook her head. "I'm online for at least three hours a day."

"I get along just fine." Or at least no one notices how broken I am.

"How are you able to work out of your home?"

"The mail works just fine." Fuller picked up the bottle and topped up their glasses. What the hell.

"It does?"

The course of this discussion was making Fuller feel like a living fossil, and it was embarrassing. "My client doesn't seem to be in hurry to receive the translations."

"No?"

"As long as they eventually arrive."

"Yeah, I guess snail mail would work in that situation." Jean must have noticed Fuller was getting upset because she now held both of his hands. Stop it, don't stop it, thought Fuller. I like this, but I'm just not sexual anymore. "I'm sorry, Stephen, it's just that I'm really surprised. It's like hearing you don't have electricity in your house."

Fuller grinned. "Then you'll be happy to know that I do have indoor plumbing."

She smiled.

He remembered how Jean always helped him to see the funny side of just about everything.

Bathurst Street and Wilson Avenue

"...it is time to re-examine all orbital data on Phobos and Demos. Our current findings appear to support Shklovsky's original hypothesis that suggested that the two moons are in actuality artificially powered structures constructed by

technologically proficient entities. In other words, they are spacecraft."

Fuller couldn't help laughing as he punched in the words on his typewriter. Those commie scientists were complete lunatics.

"Direct examination of these interplanetary, possibly interstellar, vehicles will not only reveal much about intelligent live elsewhere in the universe but their power sources will likely offer manifold solutions to current energy shortages on our world..."

Fuller had a personal theory about much of what he read. Working under such intellectually repressive conditions must have occasionally made these Soviet scientists to go crazy every once in a while. Fuller definitely knew that there was life elsewhere in the universe but he also suspected that there was no way that the Russians would have been aware of it.

"...With unlimited fusion and/or ion power freely available to all, the avenue to complete collectivization of the human race will finally be open..."

That is, unless they were all drug addicts.

But you had to love it, Fuller thought as he continued typing. For thousands of pages it would be completely sensible science, very objective, very careful, and very methodical. Then they'd go off the rails and take a little ride in the Marxist-Hegelian Delusional Theme Park. Very silly stuff, but it seemed to keep Fuller's mind in gear.

Yesterday had been great. He'd enjoyed his dinner date with Jean, and they'd agreed to meet again next week. In addition to that, they'd opened a new PharmaSave up in Downsview, and he'd scored an easy two hundred tablets from people who'd never seen him before.

Today was a good day too. The current batch of papers was getting increasingly entertaining. Some of the prehistoric Russians were arguing that certain cold viruses were in truth invading intellects from another galaxy.

Invasion of the Dirty Handkerchiefs.

What a wacky world those Soviet scientists must have lived in, not like Fuller's rather ordinary and boring routine. His bathroom door started glowing. Mr. Bruce was coming back for another visit. Fuller's day was about to go downhill.

Mimico Avenue and Lakeshore Boulevard

The joy of sex is not the only thing to go with when you consume over 688 grains of codeine a day. You can still taste your food, but it doesn't taste particularly good.

So why the hell was he at the far southwest end of town sitting in some greasy spoon? Oh yes, liver and onions.

From his pre-opiate life Fuller knew they made really good liver and onions here. Most of the people he knew back then thought liver and onions was really disgusting and particularly the way it was prepared in truck stop joints like this. Not Fuller; L&O was his number one comfort food.

God knows, he could use some comfort right now. His first reaction after waking up from last night's session with Mr. Bruce was to double his morning dose to twenty tablets, declare a unilateral moratorium on all translation and go back to bed. Instead, he left a voice message with Jean, took the bus, then the subway and then the streetcar to the Canadiana restaurant and ordered some liver and onions with a large side of mashed potatoes.

Mr. Bruce must have found Fuller particularly juicy last night because he stuck needles in his armpits, his needles, up both his nostrils, and, of course, a really big one up his ass and a long thin titanium tube up his urethra. That last one was especially painful.

"I wonder why I've never owned a computer," Fuller muttered softly as the fluids started leaking out of him.

"Probably the same reason you don't have any friends anymore and haven't spoken to anyone in your family for over a decade." Mr. Bruce sat down and slid a Star Trek movie into the VCR. It was the first in the series so Fuller knew he was in for a long night's draining. "You're a nice guy, and you're trying to limit the number of co-dependents in your life."

"Co-dependents?" The main reason Fuller talked to Mr. Bruce during these sessions was that it provided a little distraction from the pain and humiliation. Stupid, really. Like sending Christmas Cards to the Grand Inquisitor.

"Co-dependents are the people whose lives you mess up because of your addiction." Mr. Bruce seemed to be reading every word of the FBI anti-piracy warning. "It's very commendable, but it means you live in a very, very small world." The music started, the title flashed on, and some Klingon battle cruisers rolled onto the screen. After a while Mr. Bruce got bored and started talking again: "That small world you inhabit is kind of a paradox, isn't it?"

Fuller had actually been getting into the special effects, so he didn't appreciate the interruption. "How's do you figure that?"

"Your situation." Mr. Bruce laughed. "Your limited lifestyle actually connects you to a near-infinite number of civilizations throughout the universe."

"You've never put it quite that way before Mr. Bruce got up, opened the refrigerator door, and helped himself to a bottle of Molsons. On the TV, Dr. McCoy was looking intense about something. "Thanks for getting some booze in the house."

"Anything to make you feel at home."

Mr. Bruce sat back down and sucked on the bottle. "Did you know that beer is considered an essential element in the cultural and cultural evolution of complex societies?"

Fuller had a sudden mental image of a family of man-apes slowly advancing on a giant can of Coors, standing against the sunrise of the ancient African savanna.

"It's true," Mr. Bruce continued. "Hunter-gatherer societies settled down to become farmers so that they could be sure of getting a regular supply of crops."

"What's that got to do with beer and cultural evolution?"

"Why do you think they wanted the crops?"

"To eat?"

"That was a fringe benefit!" Mr. Bruce laughed. "They wanted the barley so they could always brew enough beer to get blasted every Saturday."

Another mental image: *Hockey Night in Babylon.*

Mr. Bruce got up and walked over to Fuller. "There's more to it of course." He slid a needle into Fuller's naval. "Intoxicants alter human consciousness. After a while things like art, literature, science, and video games start to emerge."

Fuller knew he should be paying very close attention because Mr. Bruce might start to make sense at any moment. However, he just wanted the needles to go away.

"These drugs produce very unique states of awareness, and we have to preserve them." Mr. Bruce gave the very small amount of flesh around Fuller's stomach a squeeze to speed up the draining.

"You never know when the Galactic Superculture is going to need them."

Stated like this, it sounded as though Fuller was contributing to something important. He suspected he really wasn't. That all this was being done to provide content for The Old Dope Channel on some interstellar specialty cable TV service.

The liver and onions arrived. The moisture around his nostrils told Fuller that he should be smelling something. At least he could remember how much he enjoyed the smell of liver and onions.

"Hi again, stranger." Jean stood next to his table. She was holding an old briefcase.

Fuller was surprised but pleased. "I didn't think you would have got my message until you got home."

"You didn't know that you can call in for voice messages?" Jean sat down and picked up a menu. "You know, you're not just an old friend, you're a digital archaeology project."

Fuller started cutting liver. "I'm not sure if I've been insulted or not."

"Oh, you're being insulted." Jean took out what looked like a plastic and crystal card from her jacket pocket. "You're shockingly behind the times."

"What's that?"

"Smart phone." Jean put the object in Fuller's

hand. "Here, catch up."

"I heard about these on CBC Radio." Fuller turned the object over and over in his hands. The icons looked like they were actually moving! "How does it work?"

"Long story." Jean peered at the slabs of fat and protein on Fuller's plate. "That looks disgusting."

"It's delicious." Fuller handed the alleged phone back to Jean. "You should try it."

Jean shook her head. "I think I'll go with the chicken Caesar."

Before Fuller could finish shrugging, Jean unzipped the briefcase and pulled out a large grey rectangle. "I hope you don't mind used gifts." She pressed a switch and the rectangle hinged open. "This is my old laptop. It's a little slow, but it does Wi-Fi."

Anywhere

Fuller's text on the glowing scree. Plus: Software that gave you sounds and moving pictures, not just words and numbers on a black background.   He never knew such stuff existed until yesterday. But wasn't stuff. Apparently, it was a whole lot of ones and zeroes doing crazy complicated things. Or it was magic dust. Hard to get his head around that.

Never mind, on to the journaling project.

Day 1

Knocked my dose down by two tablets. Mr. Bruce came by and did his usual thing. He left in time for me to get on line for a while.

Day 12

Down by four tablets per dose. Got the runs, which is a

drag, but it's been worse in the past. Must remember to wear dark pants this week. Found a site on that internet thing that talked about taking activated charcoal and magnesium tables to reduce the impact of opiate withdrawl.

Mr. Bruce was a no-show.

Day 29

Down eight tablets. I'm almost within the recommended dosage on the bottle. Mr. Bruce dropped by. He didn't seem particularly happy with what he got.

Day 52

Doing six pills a day. Just enough to control the brown stains on the underpants. Mr. Bruce came by three times this week. Extremely pissed and not at all pleased with the samples.

Got my profile up on Facebook.

Day 81

Just two pills a day. Mr. Bruce was furious, told me I failing to meet my obligations to intergalactic civilization. I didn't know it was possible to slam a space-time warp, but he seemed to manage it on his way out through my wall.

Fired my translation agency. I'm getting more work on my own these days.

Day 200

Haven't seen Mr. Bruce in quite a while. Don't know where he is. Don't want to know, and I hope he's unemployed.

No pills for weeks now. Hope that continues. Jean agreed to marry me, but we have to live at her place.

Went to the drug store. Bought some toothpaste and vitamin B. And nothing else.

The Terror of the Threshold

Abigail Wildes

How sweetly tucked the child
A powdered scent so mild,

Drifting in and out of sleep
Through innocence of dreams to keep.

But over by an icy window
Formed a beast from out the shadow.

Slowly amassing more it's form
It's hallow voice was far, forlorn.

Eyes blood red and fangs of white
Crawled it's way from Hell at night.

A weight far darker than the black
It's movement made no creek, no crack.

Hovering like fog above
Stalking 'pon the precious dove.

Acid dripped from wanting lips

To devour her in little bits.

Monstrous fingers, long and slim
Did pin the child's every limb.

Wrapped the sleeping babe in dark
Would strangle out that little spark.

The air inside small lungs compressed
While on her life it pushed and pressed.

The babe to grow a deathly pale
And close to cross the thinnest vale.

But somewhere in her stillest heart
A light awakened with a start--

A power rose, slight, smoldering
And fought against the evil being.

Threw it off her sunken chest
Till breath soared through the tiny breast.

Across the room beast snarled and screamed
As the child's life fully redeemed.

The threshold under foot gave way
The girl no longer in the sway.

Back to Hell the daemon swallowed
In agony it returned to wallow.

The fiend defeated, girl won her life
Yet so scarce aware of greatest strife.

No damaged showed on velvet skin
This war was fought so deep within.

And fluttered open her eyes of gray.

An Incident in Cain's Mark

L. Joseph Shosty

Whosoever made so callow a statement as houses being nothing more than cleverly arrayed piles of brick and timber was a fool. Consider, then, that a house is built with reverence and consecrated in the emotions of its inhabitants. Is such a thing, then, merely a sum of its parts, once such powerful metaphysical traits are applied? No, certainly not. A house takes as part of itself the collective soul of its owners. It shares in their joys, weeps in their sorrow, holds close in their fears. These things permeate the brick and eventually supplant the mortar. Similarly do they treat the timber, as tar or creosote, until the house's fate is inexorably tied with the spirits of those who reside within.

So it goes for generation upon generation. If a house is built upon love and joy, it shall seem to stand eternally in sunshine, with gentle breezes, and on crisp autumn days it shall delight with its nature. Similarly, a house built upon woe becomes a black thing, a place where cruel storms find purchase and never seem to leave, for whom it is always the deepest, bitterest winter, and the time is always midnight.

Such houses take on lives of their own, and afterward need no inhabitants to work their cruelties. Such is the legend. Such is the belief. And while a house may seem a bottomless repository for memories and emotions, sometimes there is something so dark and brutal even its well-appointed walls cannot contain it, a curse writ so large it swallows a town, perhaps even a county, and throws all into gloom. Such curses become the stuff of tales to be whispered of in the firelight or in the public house while the wind howls outside, to be cured by stout drink and a warding hand, for these are the blackest things which skulk in the night, and as such they come to us in tales that know no particular moment in time.

It is such a tale I now wish to tell.

No train passed near Cain's Mark, and having no motorcar I walked the thirty-two miles from the university, a pack slung over my shoulder. On the village outskirts I found a boarding house with rooms to let. The owner was a severe woman in a flowery blue dress which should have looked cheerful, but did not. She asked my business with one eye squinted.

"My uncle was Parsival Koenig," I said. "He passed away last week."

She raised her chin at me, a defensive pose. "I knew your uncle," she said. "He stayed here, in fact. You can have his room while you're with us." She made to show me upstairs, but then stopped. "There is no credit on his account, you understand. All monies shall be due up front."

"I understand. Where are his effects?"

"He had little with him. He was a traveler, same

as you. You'll likely find them with our constable, or the undertaker. I can't be sure which. In case you're of a mind to go find them, dinner is at five sharp. Anyone arriving at my table so much as one minute late is not welcome. A man who can't be prompt to his own feeding must make his own luck in that regard."

I nodded. "Understood. I'll be quick, then."

I settled my baggage, paid a week's rent, and thanked the woman for her help. Having done so, I pressed deeper into the village, asking the undertaker's location from a barber leaning a straight-backed chair against the wall outside his shop. He directed me two streets over, and I met with the undertaker just as he was closing shop for the afternoon.

He showed me to a room filled with caskets, those empty and those currently occupied filling the same space. He brought me to one that had already been shut and sealed.

"Here he is," the undertaker said. "Or rather, what's left of him. I suspect you'll want to arrange transport?"

"Yes," I said. "My grandmother wishes he be buried in the family plot at our ancestral home in Pennsylvania. She's instructed me to inform you she'll pay whatever price, within reason, to ensure this occurs."

"Olaf Swein's truck makes the journey to Cutler once every two weeks. They've a branch line there."

"And how soon before Mr. Swein makes his next trip?"

"Your grandmother can expect delivery by the middle of next week."

"No sooner than that? She's not accustomed to waiting, my grandmother."

"Impatience is something which runs in your family, no doubt."

I smiled. "I'm afraid so."

"It's like that with the wealthy, old families."

"I like to think I've escaped that trap."

The undertaker's brow darkened. "We'll see."

"Was my uncle impatient?" I asked.

"Yes. Indeed, he was. I knew him only a short while, but this was a trait immediately noticeable about him."

"Listen, there is some speculation about the nature of his death. Could you perhaps shed some light?"

The undertaker's posture changed. He had been a dour, rough man to start, but when I asked after what had befallen my uncle he stiffened as though carved from petrified wood. His eyes narrowed, and he said to me, "Don't meddle in such things, boy. You're a nice enough chap, but you've got the stink of the university on you. In old places such as this village, scholarly curiosity is a curse of blood. You wish to know the means of your uncle's death. Well, I'll tell you: he died because he was a fool. Break your curse and get yourself away from here before you end as he did."

"Please, I need to know more!"

The undertaker rubbed his hands together as though washing them beneath a tap. The action of skin upon skin made a dry, rasping noise. "I've done my duty," he said. "I'm obliged no further in this matter. See yourself out; I have business elsewhere."

He turned, then, and left. I did as told and

returned to the street.

My uncle's business was concluded, but I could not escape the notion that I had stumbled onto something extraordinary. I resolved to inquire further, after I had satisfied my personal reasons for coming to Cain's Mark. It was true Grandmother had dispatched me here to handle our family's affairs, but it was also true I had begged for the task. Though I was closest, geographically-speaking, I was also one of the lesser grandsons, one who had shown no interest in business or politics, instead preferring to study folklore at a small university, far from all matriarchal control. But at my insistence Grandmother agreed, and I had come. Seeing to my uncle's remains was little more than perfunctory to me. I had hardly known the man. He was a wanderer, a chaser of oil across the Southwest and California. I wondered what had brought him here, but that was hardly why I had come.

I wandered the streets of Cain's Mark until I found my real destination. It was a large mansion in the Gothic style, crumbling now from the assault of years, neglect, and the sea air. Several of its windows were cracked, and the front door hanged precariously on its hinges. Scorch marks blackened the doorway and parts of the front facing the street.

This was Sallow House.

I'd read a vague record of its purported haunting obtained from one August Sibley. The report had been made while the man was locked in an upstate asylum for the disturbed. He had ranted and raved an account of the darkness howling like mad dogs, and lived under near-constant sedation due to the violence of his hysteria while lucid. I'd read this account my freshman year and wanted to question him further. However, he expired from heart failure before I could see him. Now, with my uncle's passing, I'd had reason enough to take leave from my duties at the university and come here, perhaps to learn for myself this tale that had, I believe in part, driven a man like Sibley to madness.

I could not suppress my glee in discovering the house for myself. That meant at least part of the story I'd read was true. The hauntings were another matter entirely, and I would investigate those claims further while here.

The day, however, was getting long, and I resolved to return to the boarding house and wait until morning when I could get a fresh start. I would tour the house first, and afterward I would take an accounting from the citizenry, if they would have me. Thus far, they had been aloof in their dealings, almost belligerent in the case of the undertaker. That might change when they discovered my intent. It had been my experience a people spoke candidly of a thing when they felt their names might find print. A number of my colleagues had played off such vanities to great effect. I planned to do the same.

I checked my fob watch and found the time just before five. I would never make it back to the boarding house in time for dinner, so I went instead to a public house off the village commons. It was a squat structure, but warm and clean. The owner, a handsome middle-aged woman, entered from the kitchen, wiping her hands on her apron. She informed me in no uncertain terms that the public house would be closing promptly at sundown, all to be had was a bowl of chowder and beer, and that only if I ate with some haste. A little disconcerted I nevertheless agreed. She returned with a bowl fraught with steam and a mug of said beer. I settled my bill, and she returned to the kitchen, not to be seen again for the duration of my meal.

I ate with the promised vigor and went out the way I had come. Evening was creeping over the rooftops, and I could feel a certain bite in the autumn air not present earlier. The nights here were to likely be bitter ones, I realized. Wishing I had brought my scarf I stuffed my hands into my jacket pockets for warmth and set off for the boarding house.

I'd rounded a corner and was heading up the main street when I became aware of a noise to my left. I turned to see the grim undertaker, beckoning to me from the shadows beneath the eaves of a flower shop. I went over to him out of curiosity, but as I approached I was taken aback at the desperate fear in his eyes.

"You fool!" he whispered to me. "You've got to the get off the streets before sundown!"

"I'm returning to the boarding house now," I said.

"It's past the edges of town. You'll never make it. Come with me."

The sheer intensity of his plea compelled me to follow. We took a swift, yet winding route through the alleys and emerged on a quiet back street where we terminated at a drab, drooping structure. This was the undertaker's home.

He ushered me inside and bade me sit. The room was swallowed in a musty gloom, so I was doubly glad when the undertaker started a fire in the hearth, which was proof as well against the rising chill. The undertaker put on an iron kettle for tea and asked if I had eaten. I confirmed I had, yet he insisted on putting butter, bread, and cheese in front of me. The meal might have seemed cheerful were the undertaker not moving in such a fit of anxiety.

"You'll stay with me tonight," he said, "and if your business keeps you here longer than a day, you are to be back at your lodgings within an hour of sundown each day. Do you hear?"

I said I did.

He nodded and brought us two steaming cups of tea. I let mine sit a while, preferring it to steep until strong. The undertaker set upon his cup immediately. His hands trembled as he brought it to his lips.

"You don't know how close you came," he said.

"Close I came to what?"

The undertaker nodded to something outside the walls of his home. "You'll hear it soon enough, and if you've the foulest luck, you might even catch glimpse. Lads like you are so done up in their curiosities they seldom see the Devil is laughing at them from the shadows. Come from the university, have you?"

"You said as much earlier." The likelihood I had just stumbled upon the very thing I was seeking dawned upon me. With some eagerness I sat forward in my chair. "Please, does this have something to do with the curse?"

The undertaker's large, sharp eyes cut from the window to me. There was a violent intensity in them, like a martinet schoolmaster who seeks to thrash all creativity and verve from his students with the cut and thrust of his yardstick. "Heard of it, have you?"

"I have," I said. "I'm a folklorist, you see, so such stories are of singular interest to me. I keep my ears sharp for such, especially tales along the Eastern Seaboard. I'm collecting them into a volume."

"Are you, now?"

"A publisher has shown interest. Look, I don't have much money, but I could certainly pay you for your troubles if you would tell me, in your own words, of the story behind the curse. The authenticity would add a significance I could not derive by merely scanning old town records. It will certainly aid me when I go into the house to study it further."

"You mustn't go into that house!" the undertaker cried and came toward me with such violence I thought surely he would strike me. He did not, but he slammed two knobby fists onto the table with such force our teacups were upset. Leaning over me he said, "You mustn't. If it will please you, I'll tell you the story of Cain's Mark, but only if you make a solemn oath on your family you'll never set foot into the house. Swear on it."

Such a declaration filled me with a terrible dread. Here I had before me a zealot, with eyes burning so brightly I could scarcely look upon them without trembling. After some effort I was able to mutter, "I do. I swear on my grandmother's good name I shall not go into Sallow House."

The undertaker nodded. "I shall hold you to that promise, young lad." He sat down then, and without a single moment of preparation launched into his tale, as though he had been ready for a great long time in its revelation.

"Whosoever made so callow a statement as houses being nothing more than cleverly arrayed piles of brick and timber was a fool," he began, and then recounted for me, word for word, the paragraphs I have appropriated in opening this tale. "Such a tale surrounds Cain's Mark. It emanates from the old Wickersham house, and it touches every soul who lives here. I cannot recall the last time I saw a native smile, but I can recall a time, now long past, when we lived without a curse around our necks."

"Wait a moment. You were alive when this alleged curse befell the village?"

"Not alleged, and yes, I was certainly here. I was a boy of twelve, and my father was the undertaker before me, so I know aspects of the story which were not known by the other children of the village."

"Then it's luck that I happened on you."

He cast me a queer glance. "Is it?" he asked.

Before I could answer, he began again. "There were two brothers at Sallow House, both of them engineers trained overseas by what must surely have been some fine German professors. There was no question as boys that they shared a certain genius for invention, but it was their formal training abroad which truly transformed them. They returned and set at once, as the rich often do, to pursuits which go beyond the every day. But these experiments were at once brilliant and practical, reflecting that Prussian ethic ingrained in their training.

"Once, not so long ago, we had electric lights in our homes. The method was different than what one sees nowadays. The brothers designed it, and it was brilliant and efficient. Since their passing the lights have fallen into disrepair, and we've done nothing to modernize.

"Bertrand was the oldest. He was a toad of a man: short, fat, always with a sheen of sweat on his forehead. He said little, preferring his books and experiments. No one paid him much heed. There is a story that our old constable, Goff, would harass Bertrand on the little man's occasional strolls through the village. He hated outsiders, Goff did, especially those on foot, loitering in the village proper. He'd pick Bertrand up and haul him to jail, thinking he was some such vagabond, and not from the best family in town. And no one would ever identify Bertrand, either. As mad as it may seem, we cared so little for him that we, too, forgot who he was or that he was around.

"It was only when his brother, Peter, would miss him at home that he would go rescue Bertrand from Goff's jail. Bertrand would yell and scream his identity for hours, and no one would believe him. Or, they would ignore him, I suppose. And Peter would come for him, laughing – Peter was always laughing – and take him home again.

"Now Peter was a different sort. I read once a description of that transcendentalist character."

"Emerson?" I offered.

"Yes, that's the one. I read an account of him once that to stand near him was to stand in sunshine. That was our Peter. He was as handsome as Bertrand was ugly. He laughed all the day long, and we laughed with him. He was a great one for the pub, as the Wickershams were a wealthy bunch, and he was always buying rounds for the lads in the afternoons and evenings. He had a passion for engineering, too, same as his brother, but if there was one thing Peter valued more, it was his vanity. Peter liked being liked. We all knew it, but we didn't think poorly of him his faults. No, we loved him. We wanted for him all the best the world had to offer because he made us feel good by feeling good himself.

"But there was an ugliness in Peter, too. Sometimes his laughter was used cruelly in the evenings when he was drunk or grew bored. But, curse us, we continued to laugh, louder than before, when his antics took on this darker bent. Maybe it was a darkness in ourselves, but we encouraged him. He never made sport of anyone important, after all. And if the subject of his sarcasm were ever to protest, he would just smile and say he meant no offense. Of course he did mean his offenses, but with Peter, we were willing to forgive anything.

"When he was not being a man about town or regaling us in the pubs with his stories, Peter worked with Bertrand. All hours of the night the Brothers Wickersham toiled in their home. There was a housekeeper, Mrs. Perkins, but she deaf and dumb and never even kept a journal of the real goings-on there. But one can imagine it. They worked primarily in electricity but built other devices as well. Their genius was hindered only by sleep and the shortcomings of the age in which they lived. When they gave the village free electricity it was a time of great celebration. We had a festival in their honor that day, and at night we lit the village and danced in the streets. Of course, the Wickershams probably electrified the town for their own ends, but that was not the point, where we were concerned. We'd been given a gift, and we loved it.

"About this time, the troubles between the two brothers began. Though it was no doubt a joint effort between them, everyone gave Peter sole credit for lighting the village. Hermit though he was, Bertrand was not oblivious to the sentiments in the streets, and, being human, he rankled at the way he had been ignored.

"In a rare appearance at the pub one evening, with Peter in attendance, Bertrand announced he planned to build an electrical man, a figure who would one day revolutionize the labor industry. The effect was the opposite of his intent. He'd imagined the people suddenly realizing his worth and showering him with the same affection they had for Peter.

"It was simple vanity, of course, but his gesture received a woefully different reception. The men in the pub began to laugh at him, and jeer. Even Peter, who knew the sheer depth of his brother's powers, had a go at Bertrand. At first, it came as a gentle mocking.

"'Oh, brother, you sound like some mad king in a storybook!' The joke wasn't all that humorous. Drunk as he was, I doubt Peter could have managed much better even if he'd had an hour to think on it. But the people, who were ready to love anything Peter said or did, broke into gales of laughter. Bertrand was horrified, and there was a betrayal in him now, what with his brother joining in the derision.

"And then the fateful part came. One of the lads at the bar said, 'Peter, you should build this electrical man and show him how it's done.' The others roared their agreement.

"Peter was quite puffed up about this. 'Perhaps I will,' he said.

"And right then you could see all the brotherly love had gone out of them, and Bertrand hated his brother with all the fury of Hell itself. Peter had thrown down the gauntlet, and there was nothing more to be said. Bertrand left then, and the people laughed him all the way out and down the street. Afterward Peter stood and posed glamorously, as if he had achieved victory already, and everyone cheered.

"In the months which followed, the brothers worked independently of each other. Horse-drawn carriages arrived at all hours, day and night, loaded with exotic materials. An insomniac walking our streets in the darkest parts of midnight could see the flickering and flashing through the attic windows where Peter worked, and we could feel the rumble and groan shake the ground from the basement where Bertrand kept his workshop."

The distant howl of a dog broke the undertaker from his narrative. He cast a furtive glance out the window. Evening was upon us. Only a soft glow of daylight could still be seen. I, who had been entranced by the tale thus far, took this opportunity to sip at my tea, which was by now perfectly steeped. When the undertaker turned his attention back to me, he was clearly quite afraid.

"We haven't much time now," he said. "I must finish this tale sooner than I had expected."

"Then by all means proceed," I said.

The undertaker took a deep breath and nodded. "Well, naturally the town was quite excited over this competition. As far as we were concerned this was nothing less than a battle of good versus evil, light versus dark, God's triumph over Lucifer's dark designs. The people cheered Peter every time he was seen in town, which was often, for though he was committed to the challenge, that did not stop his coming to bask in our adulation every afternoon. Naturally, this likely hindered his research more than it helped. Who knows how it might have turned out, if he had stuck fast to his work instead of indulging his passions?"

The undertaker, whose eyes were glazed in recollection of things past, snapped suddenly back to the present, smiling ruefully. "And you see, there I go. Even after all these years, we're still making excuses for him."

"I take it he failed to beat his brother," I said.

The undertaker nodded. "Not that we didn't assist him. Bertrand still got out from time to time for a walk through the commons, no doubt to clear his head. During one of his walks through town Goff, who by now surely had to know Bertrand by appearance, locked him up, same as always, only this time Peter did not arrange for Bertrand's release, not for days, in fact. Boys broke into the house and tried to sabotage Bertrand's work, but he kept his basement so tightly secured they couldn't get in. What they did instead was deface Bertrand in the family portraits and set a fire in the kitchen which almost killed Mrs. Perkins, the dumb servant.

"One night the men gathered at the pub, and Peter was there, regaling them of his adventures in Germany, when the door opened and Bertrand appeared. He was haggard. His hair was unkempt, and it was apparent he had not bathed in some time. His nails were long and needed cutting, and he had a madness to him, a gleeful madness, which he turned on the townsfolk. He met every gaze with such a terrifying fever people were forced to look away in fear or shame. He cried out a single word, 'Success!'"

and then he was gone.

"Everyone was flabbergasted, but then, a moment later, into the pub stepped a creation of the most terrible nightmare. It was eight feet tall, so large it had to stoop to enter, made of brass that shone like gold. Far from being a clunky beast, it was lithe and delicate, nimble even, for it moved with the grace of a dancer. Surely this was a vision of the Devil, of Lucifer the Morningstar, for the thing was also so beautiful it was difficult to look upon without shedding tears.

"It smiled at the men where Bertrand had only scowled, bowed once, and then proceeded to dance a jig as if it were born to do it. All eyes looked upon it in horror. Peter slumped in his chair, all wit and witticism having fled. The electric man finished its dance and disappeared again without another word.

"All was left in stunned silence until someone spoke up. Being only a lad at the time and relying mostly on the accounts of my father, I don't know who first suggested it. However, there came forth words of outrage and delusion.

"'How dare he?' someone cried.

"'Shame!' cried another.

"'Yes,' Peter replied.

"'Peter, that is yours!'

"'Yes.' By now Peter was lost in the dark corridors of thought. The others must have sensed it, for they certainly goaded him onward.

"'He's stolen your device from you. Yours!'

"'Yes.'

"'Don't let him claim the fruits of your hard work!'

"Peter sprang from his chair. 'Yes!' he cried, and

he left at once to confront his brother.

"Word of their imminent reckoning spread across the village, and the people turned out in the streets in hopes of catching some sign or word of the victor. After this night we knew there could be only one Wickersham. We had given a Peter a mandate of blood, you see. The people still wanted greatness for him and would do virtually anything to continue their delusion, but Bertrand's triumph had shamed Peter and in turn shamed the citizenry of Cain's Mark, who had supported and even assisted him. They would willingly continue to believe whatever was necessary to make Peter great, but he must atone by stamping out the shame.

"Peter certainly showed great enthusiasm for it. He charged into Sallow House and confronted his brother. No one knows exactly what occurred. Shouts could be heard from the street, and on occasion there did come the sounds of crockery shattering as though being dashed against the wall. We were filled with an awful anticipation.

"Finally there came a single gunshot, and all was silent. Looks were exchanged on the street; a nervous twitter was about. Was it over, we asked?

"The nervousness changed slowly to calm assuredness. 'Peter had done it,' someone pronounced, and there were nods. Good! To finally be rid of the monster, Bertrand!

"But when the door opened, a ragged ghost of a character emerged. Exuberance died on our lips. It was Bertrand. He stepped onto the porch with a revolver in his hand. A smear of blood adorned his shirt, and we knew then he had bested Peter again.

"A wail rose up from the crowd. This was too

much. Were we the Jews of ancient times we might have torn our mantles and slapped our faces in outrage. Here was our devil before us, having offended us once by building what his brother could not, and now he stood before us again, defiantly refusing to die to assuage our anguish. The notion of his evil was clear to us, and it should have been to him. Clearly, he should have known his lot was to die so his brother might claim his success. Instead, he tossed the revolver to the ground and spat at us. This was too much.

"A man named Brawley was sent for. He lived outside the village and was known to keep a pack of intemperate hounds. The dogs came bristling and howling into the village proper, Brawley wrestling and cursing them. Some men then went into the house and dragged forth Bertrand. He fought with a feral savagery and spewed curses of his own. The men took turns hitting him, hoping to beat the words from his lips, and they threw him to the dogs, who went mad at the sight of him and attacked."

The undertaker lowered his head into his hands. "They tore him apart," he whispered. "After they had laid him out in my father's parlor, and Father had gone to drink a pint or two before he set to his grim work, I snuck in and saw what had become of Bertrand. It was horrible beyond imagining. I'll take the image of him lying there to my grave, and I'll never share a word of it with anyone.

"And anyway, he wasn't left to sit long. My father returned and made fast work of him. Why he was brought to my father to begin with remains unclear to me, unless it was out of mere habit. He drained Bertrand of his blood, as was custom, and cleaned the body, but he did not prepare it for burial. By and by, men came and carted Bertrand's remains off to the woods, where they presumably left them in the open to be devoured by scavengers.

"Conversely, Peter was taken from Sallow House with great ceremony, carried on the shoulders of eight men who led him in procession to my father's parlor. Later, he was given the most elaborate of funerals. The people grieved his loss, and they missed the free rounds at the pub. Mostly, I believe, they missed the promise he'd shown, the promise both had shown. At least, that's what I hope of them."

"But wait," I said, "what about the, uh, thing Bertrand created. The electric man. What became of it?"

"No one knows. You see, the following Easter the curse appeared. It took us by surprise, and many fell to it. At a most desperate point, someone tried to burn the house. You've no doubt seen the scorch marks. One of the Wickershams had shrewdly coated the wooden frame with a substance that wouldn't allow fire to catch hold. Very clever, given the nature of their experiments. But before the fire died out, it was quite bright and dramatic. The electric man, who had been all but forgotten by then, ran from the house to escape the fire. A man died from the fright of seeing him again. Potter was his name. He was the first man I helped my father prepare and bury. No one could catch the electric man. He fled from us when we gave chase, stopping at the village edge and doing that awful, damnable dance of his to mock us before disappearing into the woods beyond. There are rumors now that he still stalks the surrounding countryside. What he does is anyone's guess."

I gulped the last of my tea.

"And the curse?" I asked. "What of it?"

He lifted a finger into the air and bade me listen. The barking and baying of dogs was louder now. So caught up was I in the undertaker's tale, I'd failed to hear their approach.

"They'll pass by here soon," the undertaker whispered. He led me to the window and opened the curtain for me to look. It did not take long. A pack of huge, black hounds tore past, their noses to the ground, jaws slavering, the horrid howling issuing from their throats. They were hunting something. I asked the undertaker what that could be.

"Every night," he said, "they come and take anyone unlucky enough to find himself on the streets after sundown. Much in the way the dogs tore apart Bertrand all those years ago, they will set upon the hapless. Man, woman, even child: the hounds know no distinction where flesh is concerned."

I peered further at them, for they were paying particular attention to our street. Something about them was extraordinary. There was a deformity to their heads, and it wasn't until one passed beneath a streetlight that I recognized it in full. My throat tightened. The hounds had human faces. The faces, perhaps, of those who had been taken. I was filled with a sublime horror and could do nothing but stare.

A figure scampered in among the hounds. It was vaguely human-shaped, yet it moved on all fours. It wore a torn black suit, filthy white shirt, and suspenders. Its body was short, stocky, its hair long and greasy, and its nails in need of cutting.

"Bertrand," I said.

"Yes. He travels with them, our very own Master

of the Wild Hunt. Do not make eye contact with him! The hounds cannot cross thresholds, but it is said to look upon Bertrand is to make an invitation. We are safe so long as you keep your eyes averted."

I did as the undertaker told me, but I was haunted by the thought of that apparition, stalking the lands at night, feasting on the unwary. My morbid curiosity begged for one more glance, but I knew that would turn into an infinitely long moment if I was so permitted, for I wanted to drink in every detail. Instead, I turned to face the undertaker, who was removed from the window. He had never peered outside, in fact, as though he were too horrified, too ashamed, even, to look upon the work of his forefathers.

"What does he search for?" I asked, but alas, the question was never answered. One of the hounds had crept to the window and stood on hind legs now, forepaws pressing against the glass. The sudden movement turned my eyes toward it, and immediately I was struck with a seizure in my chest. I fell backward onto the floor, and I began to scream. For how long, I cannot say, but when the undertaker finally shook sense into me again, I could not speak for a long while, despite his coaxing.

"What is it, lad?" he asked me. "What is it?"

"The hound," I whispered at last. "The one at the window." My cheeks, I could only imagine wore the deathly pallor of chalk. "Its face! Its face!"

I did not sleep that night. In the morning I made the proper arrangements to ship my uncle's remains to my family estate, and I planned to make my way home again to the university. My feet, however, would not set homeward of their own accord. I was still too shaken by what I had seen the night before. Further, the lands which had been so bright and cheerful on my journey to Cain's Mark now seemed darker, more fraught with unknown things which lurked just outside the corner of the eye.

I paid the fellow Swein an obscene sum to drive me to the nearest station, where I purchased a ticket back home again. It wasn't until I had reached the safety of my dorms that I felt the specter of Cain's Mark relent, if only slightly.

But leave me entirely it has not, for the points of the undertaker's tale haunt me still. I have never recounted my experiences until now, and I speak of it now only because I hope a record of Cain's Mark shall lift from me the feeling of pure horror that has me in its hoary grip. As such, I am dictating it to a friend, who has been kind enough to humor a madman and continue on diligently, no matter what absurdity might reach his ears.

I do not know what else to do. If some relief is not given me soon, I shall surely perish. If this does not work, I'm afraid despair will crush my bones. For I cannot shake the image of what I saw that night as the hound stood looking at me through the window. All I had seen and heard up to that point had frightened me, to be sure, but it was an exhilarating thing, as I was so far removed from the curse. Yet, as I gazed upon the creature who stared at me, with mad, hate-filled eyes, broken teeth bared and desiring my blood, I knew at a primal level I was no further removed from the curse than the undertaker, for here, before me, was a hound who wore the face of my uncle. May God have mercy upon all our souls!

Spiral

Don Webb

The nostrums of this shop, reflected Beyer, were incredibly old. Traditional botanica--rosemary, uva ursi, southernwood, vetiver--mingled with those substances the FDA had relegated to the rank of modern voodoo: DMSO, procainamide HCl, apricot seed extract. Beyer had heard the owner of this unlikely shoppe had discovered a secret cache of the near-fabulous Orange Sunshine.

Seeking the Grail, Beyer walked past the yellow and day-glow orange eye-in-the-pyramid sign and into the dimly lit shop on the Rue d. Dragon. Cassilda's was not far from the gin-smelling Rue d. Bourbon. Beyer had had some difficulty in finding the address in the maze of the Crescent City. Now waiting in the gloom, he watched the approach of an aged crone through a beaded curtain.

Beyer had expected a young, born-again neopagan--a follower of the demidivines Pan and Leary. This crone resembled the dried mumia whose dusty powders no doubt lay on a half-forgotten shelf in this shop.

"Can I help you, young man?"

"I was looking for something special, something enlightening."

"Our botanica has many aids for those questing in the mystic arts. This mandrake, for instance, has helped many find the Inner Light."

"I was looking for something a little more... synthetic."

She stared at Beyer intently, fingering a curiously wrought thunderbird she wore over her dingy shop smock. She lifted her right eyebrow in the time-honored tradition of Leonard Nimoy.

"You'd not be police, then? Follow me." The shrunken hag glided through the glass bead curtain into an even darker area. Beyer followed, smelling the cloying mix of both patchouli and rot. The inner sanctum was conventional New Orleans Voudon. Pictures of saints, of Hindu gods, of various arcane symbols graced the walls. Candles of all colors filled the room; many were incised with the symbols on the walls but did nothing with their light to shake off the gloom. To Beyer's disgust, many of the candles were scented, pouring out their own poisons into the ever-thickening atmosphere. He would have preferred the industrial smokestacks of his native New Jersey.

The crone was unfastening a red lacquered Chinese box that was riddled, like others of its species, with secret catches and caches. From one of these she produced a sheet of purple-imprinted blotter paper.

"That's not exactly what I came for."

"It's what I've got."

The paper was printed neither with dragons, stars, unicorns, nor cartoon figures--all of which Beyer was familiar with. Instead, each hit bore the imprint of a double-headed ax--no, a double-headed ax-shaped maze. The sheet held ninety-three hits.

"How much?"

"Three dollars each. In lots of ten or more, two dollars."

"Where is it from? I've never seen blotter like this."

"Aye, and you be a crafty one. Finest made. Hoffman would dream of such as this. It's from a place you not be likely to be going from. Celephais. Each one bears the labyris seal of approval." The crone gave an eerie laugh. Beyer wondered how she had sneaked out of *Macbeth*.

"I'll take the lot."

The acid was folded into a red flannel bag. "Comes with every purchase of five dollars or more."

Beyer said, "You're not really what I expected."

"Cassilda Jones has been selling enlightenment for a long time. Best hurry home, my boy, 'fore the showers ketch you."

Beyer went into the sunny street. As the old woman had said, a freak Gulf storm drenched him before he made it back to his hotel. With the self-sacrifice a bibliophile gives to his books, Beyer kept his precious acquisition from getting wet.

Beyer showered, then sat on his bed and watched *The Black Cat*, an old black-and-white movie with Boris Karloff. He was going to spend the afternoon relaxing. Later that evening he would go to hear Preservation Hall jazz and drop three hits. When the Hall closed, he would wander through the lineal labyrinth of Rue d. Bourbon. This was an annual ritual: an escape from his prosaic accounting job in Trenton.

When evening came he dressed in an outrageous set of glad rags--a canary yellow three-piece suit, white silk shirt, black wingtips, and the crowning glory of a maroon fedora. Beyer decided to catch a quick meal at the Three Sisters before tripping off to Preservation Hall.

The setting sun had turned the sky a saffron no more believable than the colors of Beyer's suit. Making his way down streets webbed with wrought iron, he caught a glimpse of Jackson Square. A knot of people were carrying signs protesting the U.S. involvement in Beliz. Watching the maypole, he lost his footing, tripped, and landed in the street between two parked cabs. To his intense annoyance he had landed in a pile of horse droppings. He stood up and began cleaning his yellow suit, wondering how horse dung had found its way into such an urban environment.

"I say, guv, that ain't ordinary dung--it's *Verfremdung*."

Beyer looked up. On the sidewalk lounged a dwarf dressed exactly as was Beyer. This diminutive parody of himself was a bit more kaleidoscopic, though, having green hair. Beyer managed to say, "What?"

"*Verfremdung*, alienation, that is to say, you're not only in the shit, you're out of it as well." The dwarf placed his finger aside his nose and vanished with a green flash. No one else was on the street, nor did the Jackson Square protesters seem to notice this untoward flash.

A few minutes cleaning had removed all trace of excrement from the jacket. A bewildered Beyer made his way to the Three Sisters. In the inner courtyard he enjoyed the cool New Orleans twilight and the hot crayfish bisque.

As he spooned up the last few rich, red drops of the bisque, Beyer saw Charlie Chan walk in. Mr. Chan was dressed, as is his wont, all in white. He was the second brightest thing in the inner courtyard, outshone only by Beyer. The world-famous detective (and sometimes Good Humor man) walked to Beyer's wrought iron table. His almond eyes impassive, he handed Beyer a fortune cookie.

As Mr. Chan left, Beyer broke open the cookie containing the Wisdom of the Ancient East: "Familiarity and strangeness are categories of one's physico-spiritual existence in three-dimensional space. And how are you tonight, Mr. Beyer?"

Mr. Beyer walked into the comforting familiarity of Preservation Hall to the tune of "East St. Louis Blues." The band was hot tonight. He ordered a dark Heineken and covertly placed three hits in his mouth. He chewed them, sloshing dark beer through his mouth like a winetaster's wine or Mr. Babbit's Listerine. To the beautifully structured "Wolverine Blues," he finally swallowed them.

He was on his third, maybe fourth, beer when he noticed the girl sitting beside him. She was dark, Grecian probably. Her hair was the black of outer space, but her eyes were lambent violet. She wore a simple shift of reddish-brown-purple of Tyre. Clasped about her neck was a massive gold torque studded with green and red garnets. Her eyes were hungry and desperate. The band was playing the "Jelly Roll Blues."

". . . He's so tall and chancy

He's the lady's fancy
He's the red hot stuff
Friend's you can't get enough
Play it short--don't abuse
Play them JELLY ROLL BLUES."

The girl spoke with a fevered intensity. "I know you can help me. I saw the royal seal. By Apollo, I didn't know there were any followers left. You must hurry--a barbarian is going to kill the Beautiful One."

"Uh, say again?" Beyer figured the stuff was really kicking in.

"The Beautiful One, Asterion, son of Phasaphae. A Greek lad from the uncouth craggy main has rearrived at the temple. Come now, oh hero of the labyris."

Beyer excused himself, going to the mens' room. The room's atmosphere had a reassuringly normal taint of urine. Beyer unzipped his fly and proceeded to baptize the porcelain with the 2-oxy-lysergic acid diethylamide-bearing piss. As he zipped up his fly, he was accosted by the dwarven clone of his earlier encounter.

The dwarf winked a knowing eye and began to soapbox.

"Mr. Beyer, if I were to adopt an idea as so many people do, and fondle it in my embraces to the exclusion of all others, it would be that the great want which mankind labors under at this present period is sleep. The world should recline its vast head on the first convenient pillow and take an age-long nap. It has gone distracted through a morbid activity, and, while preternaturally wide awake, is nevertheless tormented by visions that seem real to it now, but would assume their true aspect and character were all things once set right by an interval of sound repose. Indeed, that which knits up--" At this moment the dwarf was struck from behind by a silver hammer, thus saving Beyer from a preternaturally long discourse.

Beyer smiled at the wielder of the mallet argent, "Thank you, Dr. Maxwell."

The world-famous physicist replied, "Nada."

Beyer said, "Don't you think that another term would balance that out?" pointing to the sinister side of an equation Maxwell was carrying. The physicist furrowed his brow but was distracted as a demon ran by. Maxwell turned, giving chase with his hammer; both he and the impish fellow from the infernal regions vanished into a toilet stall.

Beyer returned to the main room. The band was playing "Shreveport Stomps." The lights of the Hall were blinking on and off to the rhythm of the music in binary synesthesia. The little Cretan girl was still there, staring at his half-finished Heineken bottle as if to summon her hero by sympathetic magic.

Beyer walked over to her, motioned her to sit while he drained his Dutch suds. They walked into the night to the accompaniment of "Grandpa's Spells."

The New Orleans night was its normal hustle. The unlikely pair walked past a crowd that was being harangued by a swarthy, turbaned evangelist: "And I sezs unto yew, my brothers and sisters, that which is not dead can eternal lie and after strange aeons Death may die. Alleluia!"

Must be a Moonie, decided Beyer, as the pair hastened through the moonlit streets and half-deserted retreats of New Orleans. They were going to a part of the city which Beyer didn't know. Once they passed a man trying to load quicksilver with a pitchfork into the bed of a green Chevy pick-em-up truck.

The wrought iron of the Crescent City was gradually being replaced by marbled architecture. Soon they stood before the big brass doors of the labyris hall.

The Cretan maid pointed to a piece of white yarn snaking its way from under the massive door. "The Greek barbarian has devised a way of insuring his path through the labyris hall and even now goes to slay Asterion, son of the Queen. Be quick, my hero, and slay this foul abomination of a goatherd. Put an end to this dissection on the march. May great Zeus, the Father of our purple-locked king, enfold thee with His aegis."

The girl opened the immense door and thrust Beyer within. It was dark and musty. Beyer made his way through the serpentine corridors, following the white thread. A figure crouched ahead in the darkness, examining the white yarn through a magnifying glass. It was Mr. Moto.

"Bought at Woolworth, just as I expected. Ah so! It is Mr. Beyer, just on time."

Beyer regarded the inscrutable Oriental. "Mr. Moto, do you have a gun I could borrow? I've gotta slay this Greek guy."

"No, Mr. Beyer, I am unfortunately unarmed. I suggest you use your wits against the Bronze Age hero. Good Ruck!" Mr. Moto bowed.

A turn to the left. Two turns to the right, past a janitor. Then Beyer saw the barbarian; a bronze sword glinted from one brawny arm. Frontal attack would prove deadly. After a brief moment's thought, Beyer raced back to the janitor.

"Say, Mac, you got a penknife?" The janitor, smiling a toothless grin, handed him a Swiss Army knife.

Beyer crept 'til he was twenty feet behind the Greek barbarian. Then he used the borrowed knife to sever the yarn. He lit it with his disposable lighter. The yarn burned with a soft pffft! When the spark reached the Greek, the barbarian exploded into a million bloody fragments. Beyer returned the knife to the janitor, now the green-haired dwarf.

"Sorry about the mess."

Beyer continued into the maze. Soon he met Asterion, the bull-headed man. The minotaur showed him to a doorway marked EXIT in Linear B script. Beyer walked through into the back room of Cassilda Jones' place.

He smiled at the old lady as he walked out onto the sunny street.

The Other Side

Kurt Newton

The Mouth heaved in the night, lapping at the dock's pylons with its thick, putrid tongue. Brayton sat on a wooden crate beside his boat, picking at his fingernails and tossing the unwanted pieces into the mist. His gondola rose and fell, scraping slightly against the side of the dock. The pylons creaked.

Footsteps.

A figure moved from out of the dark into the scant light thrown by one of the sealed lamps that dotted the wharf. A man dressed in a second-hand trench coat, wearing a black knitted cap, approached.

"Mr. Brayton?"

Brayton stood. "You can drop the 'mister.' You got the money?"

The man pulled an envelope from his coat pocket and handed it over. "Five-thousand, correct?"

Brayton weighed the envelope in his hand. Old money: it was as good as gold used to be.

Satisfied, Brayton pocketed the envelope without counting its contents. "Climb aboard." The man in the trench coat brushed past him, stepped down into the boat and settled onto the front seat.

Brayton knew that underneath the man's coat was an expensive designer suit; underneath the knitted cap was a hundred-dollar haircut. The man likely had several money belts wrapped around his midsection, in direct defiance to the old adage that you can't take it with you. Brayton had seen the lot of them: men of high position escaping jail-time for embezzlement and extortion, running from the grasp of vengeful business partners, or avoiding the scandal of indiscretions; illegally crossing the Mouth to get to the other side, to start life fresh, guilt-free. Or so they believed.

Brayton took his place at the stern. He leaned over the side rail and unhooked a thick rope. Using a long pole, he pushed off from the dock. The gondola's narrow nose turned toward open water.

"Open water"--a term used loosely for the Mouth. In reality, it was an undulating debris field floating atop the surface of the moat-like body of water, home to the city island's waste, decay, and secrets. It was too thick for motorized transportation; propellers simply churned to a halt. It was suicide to try and swim across. Those desperate enough quickly became part of the Mouth, so called because it was believed that all that entered the Mouth was swallowed down. Everything, that is, except the gondolas. Using pole and oar, the gondoliers managed to navigate the deadly obstacle course with an ease that was a mystery to most, and a Godsend for some.

Brayton plunged the single oar into the water and gently fishtailed it. The iron-shielded prow plowed through the debris ahead. A creaking, rhythmic calm soon descended. As the mist thickened, the minimal lighting at the dock and the cumulative glow of the city island faded from view. Ahead lay only darkness.

As Brayton navigated, he didn't know if he could truly see in the dark or if his vision was simply the product of repeated journeys mapped across a mental landscape. It didn't matter. It was just one of many incongruent details he pondered during his time alone with the Mouth. What mattered was delivering his passengers to the other side.

Oil drums, plastic containers, wooden crates with rope netting and buoys still attached, scraped against the boat's ribs. Not far from shore, the thick odor of a rotting corpse hovered like a cloud, prompting Brayton's passenger to pull a handkerchief out of his coat pocket and cover his nose and mouth. The smell was accompanied by the scuttling of crabs fighting each other for a meal. Brayton breathed the decay into his lungs as he would any other breath. Stagnant seawater, rotted fish, dead bodies; like the absence of light, he was used to it.

His passenger kept silent, eyes staring ahead into the dark, into the unknown. There was nothing to say. The weight of the occasion spoke for itself. But the silence would soon become its own weight, one too heavy to bear. Until then, Brayton had only the mist and the task at hand for company.

His arms worked the narrow-bladed oar. With each down-stroke he felt the Mouth give then begin to take, sucking at the oar like a spoon. Brayton applied pressure, pivoting the oar in the forcola, rotating it upward until it was free again. He had repeated this movement so many times he no longer needed to think about, his muscles responding with a memory of their own.

The boat lurched. The gondola's prow deflected

roughly off something large in the water. In the blindness of the moment, Brayton's passenger was at last stirred to speak.

"How do you know where you're going?"

Brayton pushed off the obstacle with the pole. "The same way I know that what we just hit was once part of the old land bridge. By memory. By touch. By the smell of the water."

The man shifted in his seat.

"If it will make you feel better, there's a portolight under your feet. But I warn you, it's best not to see what's ahead of you."

The man sat for a moment. The boat lurched again and an animal-like squeal penetrated the night. The man bent and fished for the portolight. After a moment of fumbling the light came on. The beam jerked wildly about until it located the source of the sound. A gasp escaped the man's throat.

Like seals bathing in the mist, creatures lay atop the floating islands of debris. Their bodies were pale and wrinkled as if they spent the majority of their existence in the dark. They stared at the light with black, unblinking eyes, their faces more pig-like than seal.

"What are they?"

Brayton continued to paddle. "Bloaters."

His passenger leaned forward as if to get a better look. When he did, two pale, spongy hands gripped the boat's edge and a creature rose up, dripping wet, from beneath the bow. It pulled itself to within inches of the man's face before Brayton wielded his push-pole and sent it crashing down on the creature's hands. An agonized squeal escaped the creature's mouth before it dropped back into the murk.

The passenger scrambled to the relative safety of the boat's middle seat, dropping the portolight. When he picked it back up he held it to his chest like a life preserver, the beam cutting through the mist into the sky like a searchlight. He turned toward Brayton, his face lit from underneath.

"They have hands...and fingers. Did you see them?"

Brayton remained in the shadows of the stern. "I told you it was best not to see what was ahead of you."

There came another scrape along the boat's belly, the sound of claws grabbing for purchase. The passenger's eyes darted toward the sound. Brayton continued his slow, rhythmic paddling, his pace unchanged. He nodded to the portolight in the man's grip. "The light attracts them," he said.

The man's face twisted as he debated whether or not to keep the light on. When the clawing sounds grew more persistent, he at last flicked the off-switch. The sounds abated, and once again there was only darkness.

The minutes floated by.

"What's your name?" Brayton asked.

"None of your damn business! Just get me to the other side." The man's voice shook.

"Got a wife?"

Silence.

"Kids?"

Still nothing. The man's body trembled as if the air had gone cold.

"The reason I ask is there are many reasons why a man chooses to leave it all behind." The paddle cut into the Mouth, producing a thick sucking sound.

"But there's only one real reason."

"Yeah, what's that?"

Brayton let the time slide by. He had nothing but time. "They're afraid."

"Afraid of what?"

"The truth."

The man laughed. "Truth?" He spoke the word as if it were something profane. "You think because you're helping me, that gives you the right to judge me? You don't know me. You don't know what I've done or didn't do. And while we're talking truth here...the truth is what you do is just as illegal as anything I might have done. Helping people escape the Island is a crime. The truth is you're no better. In fact, you're worse. You're what we call in the business a bottom feeder."

Brayton stopped paddling. Before the man could react, Brayton had the portolight in his hand; its long white beam cut through the night.

"What are you doing?" the man asked.

As the gondola drifted, splashes sounded on both sides of the boat.

"Turn it off!"

The first bloater reached the starboard side in seconds and pulled itself up.

"Turn it off, I said!" The man pulled a gun from his jacket and pointed it at Brayton. "I'll use it!"

"No, you won't."

In a flash of movement Brayton brought the end of his push-pole up under the man's wrist, sending the gun flying overboard. The man stared at his hand as if it had betrayed him.

"Tell me what you did," offered Brayton, "and I'll turn the light off."

"Why, you fucking piece of shit."

A second bloater grappled to get inside the boat. The man shifted first one way then the other, until his body at last gave up movement and he stood frozen in place. "All right, all right! Take care of them, and I'll tell you."

Brayton wielded his push-pole like a Japanese bō, sending the first bloater back into the water with a blow to the sternum. He then pivoted, and with a short but effective thrust to the side of the second creature's skull, it too was sent into the water.

As before, Brayton calmly resumed his position at the stern and the boat was moving again. He switched the light off. "Time to confess."

The passenger slumped in his seat and stared into the mist ahead. "It began simply..."

It always does, thought Brayton.

"I wanted to succeed. I worked hard. I paid my dues. I sold bread as a kid, bread I'd scavenged from the dumpsters behind the Island's high-rise restaurants. I swept floors, I ran errands—you name it. I made enough money to buy a hot-synch stand. Soon I was in contact with certain people who knew certain people in high places. I got a basement apartment inside the Wall, met a nice girl, and raised a family. I literally clawed my way up out of the streets and into the high-rises, above the mist, above the stench. And then I killed a man."

Brayton waited. The Mouth waited. Only the gondola continued to move, sliding across the surface of the water as the passenger gathered his thoughts.

"I owed a lot of favors to a lot of people. One was to a couple of sharks on the street. It was a simple collection down by the docks. Some young fool who was in way over his head. I was just supposed to scare him, maybe break a finger or two. But the kid started swinging. Before I knew it, I'd pulled my gun. The kid grabbed my wrist and the gun went off. Hit one of the sharks right in the chest. The other shark reached into his jacket, so I shot him too. In the business, nobody cares how things happen; they just care how things look. That dumb-ass kid had signed my death warrant.

"That's when the kid began pleading for his life. He told me he had a wife and baby and all that, and he was sorry about what had just happened. He would find a way to pay me the money. Nobody would have to know, he kept saying. Well, I knew. And I had to protect my own, even if it was just for a little while. The kid's eyes haunt me to this day."

The gondola slowed. The passenger was too enraptured with his own confession to realize the boat had slowed until it had stopped completely.

"What's going on?"

"Get out," Brayton said.

The man stood. "Have we reached the other side?"

"No. Get out."

"But I don't understand. I told you the truth." The man didn't even see the push-pole coming toward him in the dark. The force of the impact sent him over the edge of the gondola. There came a heavy splash, followed by quick gasps. Brayton grabbed the portolight and shined its wide beam on the water.

The man clung to a piece of wreckage from a rooftop glider. His knit hat had come off revealing a balding pate. The Mouth sucked at the hem of his trench coat, pulling him down. "I confessed!" the man shouted. "God dammit, I confessed!"

"You did, and that counts for something." Brayton plunged the oar into the water and began to turn the gondola around. "But truth is a funny thing. The truth is you're out here, and the damage you've caused is back there. The truth is you chose what was easy over what was right."

There came a distant splash in the dark. A bloater. In the mist, it was difficult to gauge just how far away it was.

"Wait! Who hired you?" the man shouted. "I'll pay you double. Triple!" The man reached under his coat and tore free one of the money belts. "Here, take it!" He flung the wet belt toward the boat but if fell short and quickly disappeared into the Mouth. "I have more. Just get me back into the boat. Please, I beg you. Don't leave me out here with *them*."

More splashes now, more bloaters entering the water. The Mouth was forever hungry.

"Wait! If I'm going to die out here, at least let me know who you are. Let me see your face!"

Brayton paused, then tipped the portolight until his head was bathed in the beam. He fought to keep his eyes from squinting; he wasn't used to looking into the light.

"You... But it can't be. You were dead."

"Nothing stays dead here for very long," said Brayton. "Nothing. You'll see." Brayton extinguished the portolight and steered the gondola quietly away... away from the squeals and the screams.

The mist once again surrounded him like a shroud.

The Mouth heaved in the night.

She Just Wants to Get High

Oliver Lodge

I ain't Daddy Warbucks or nothin', but I was thinking I could swing dinner and a movie this coming weekend. Is that old-fashioned? No, folks still do that. Unfortunately, in this woman's case, she only wants to get high.

I finally got her number. She texted me to tell me it's her day off tomorrow. Could I front her a bundle until she gets paid on Friday? She just wants to get high.

I picked her up at the motel. Her "headquarters" as she called it. She got into the passenger seat and emptied out an industrial-sized Ziploc filled with enough baggies of meth to send Rockefeller himself to prison along with the two of us for a solid twenty years. Under the plastic, the crystal shards glittered in the morning sun.

I heard somewhere that methamphetamine releases ten times as much dopamine as an orgasm. Ten fucking times! *If only I had what those drugs have to offer,* I thought. *Women would swoon at the very mention of my name. They would fall at my feet in awe of this almighty Casanova dispatched from the heavens to save womankind. My female disciples would kneel before me and kiss my toes. They would worship the giant pulsing rod between my legs pointing skyward, believing it to be a symbol of infinite power.*

"This is all I have ever wanted ever since I shot speed for the first time," my passenger reflected with stars in her eyes. "Enough glass to last me an eternity!'

Her eyes were dilated. Pinpoints of child-like rapture glistened in the center of those wide, blackened orbs. Sores were just starting to blossom on her creamy, young skin. I wish I could have cured her of this happy malady by sucking the pus from them like the dogs that came to Lazarus in the Bible, the lysozymes in my saliva erasing every positive association and craving for the drug one lick at a time. I wish I could have saved her from the clutches of this all-absorbing adulation. But I knew I was no match for her psychotropic hero. A toddler would have a better chance of beating Tyson in the ring. But I chanced to tell her that I loved her all the same.

"I know you do," she said. "And it means something. It really does. Problem is, I just want to get high."

I called her later that night. Through the tinny grate of the speaker against her ear, I made this proclamation: "I can make you higher than any of that garbage you've been shooting. I'm better than all that stepped-on coke and those shitty "e" pills. I'll drive over to you through this ugly snowstorm right this minute to prove it. I'll burst through that ramshackle door when I get to your place and shove you up against the wall. I'll completely swallow that succulent pink tongue of yours and send you into fits of unbearable ecstasy with my caresses. I will set your brain alight with an implosion of firing synapses, conjuring up a neurochemical blizzard of intense euphoria when I go down on you, keeping my head between your thighs until you beg me to stick it inside you. A tornado of endorphins will surround us within the hothouse of our lust. I will make you projectile squirt as I hammer my cock into your tight, wet, little box. Your ejaculate will be dripping off the ceiling like a tsunami crashing over on top of your roof. Then we will collapse beside one another as gallons of oxytocin--sticky and swelling with sweetness--come dribbling through the cracks and fissures of your battered bedroom. The best thing about it is that it's all natural, it's great for your health, and there's no hangover in the morning."

"That sounds all well and good," she responded. "But I just want to get high."

My best friend went over to her place the next night. He didn't have to jump through any of the hoops I did. He had some crack and some money so she let him fuck her. It was because she just wanted to get high.

"Has she no heart? No shame?!" I asked myself. No, I was reading into it too deeply. She just wants to get high.

"How about when we first met?" I asked her. "You said that maybe we could get clean together. We could support each other. You read me some of your most heartfelt poems, and we wrote down affirmations we would recite together every morning to reinforce the importance of sticking to our goals of staying sober."

"Intentions and actions are two very different things," she responded. "At the time I thought it sounded like a possibility, but then I realized that you were kind of an asshole and lapsed into my old ways."

I came over to sell her some drugs a few nights later. I couldn't keep my eyes open or sit up straight at the kitchen table. My cigarette had burned down to the filter between my fingers. She could tell I had done too much dope. "What I tell you about nodding out in front of the baby?" she screamed.

I stammered an apology and took out the oxycodone she had purchased. I failed to notice that a few of the tiny, green pills had fallen out of my coin pocket and onto the linoleum floor where her two-year-old was playing. He thought they were candy and ate them. He went into a coma. He lasted a week in the hospital before he died. His mother knew I had dirt on her so she didn't give me up to the police.

I thought she would never speak to me but received a call from her a month after the funeral. She knew it was late but wanted to know what I could get her in terms of "dry goods". I had exactly what she had been looking for and brought it over. She was completely shit-faced. She had lost a lot of weight. She wasn't mad at me for some reason. Even though it was a sore subject, I thought it would be callous of me not to ask her how she was handling the death of her son.

"He was my everything. I can't believe he's gone," she sobbed. "I will never get over the loss. Now I *need* to get high!"

We started to hang out again, but it didn't work out. She wanted no part of me unless I could get her stoned. I got to feeling used. We constantly argued about it.

She blocked me on her phone for the twentieth time. Three months passed, and I still couldn't get through to her. She wasn't fucking around this time. It was over between us. She hated me. I heard she was looking pretty rough around the edges. I wanted to love her, but getting fucked up was more important to her. I got mad at her and said the most horrendous shit to the poor girl. Called her a low-life whore...told her she was a worthless piece of shit. But she really can't be blamed for anything. It wasn't like I wasn't getting high with her. But then I wanted to do more than just get high for a change. I've been clean for almost eight months now. I still smoke weed and drink every once in a while. But I don't consider weed a drug.

Her? Still to this day, all she wants to do is get high.

Visitation

Dona Fox

I'm addicted
to the sulfur
curling in her wake.
Delicious, cloying
sweetness,
reminiscent that
She lives.
Men would deride
my little sports,
She rewards
each death
with visitation.

Damnation By Degrees

Paul Lubaczewski

Welcome to my little moral tale. Pleased to make your acquaintance. Oh, my name? I'm afraid my real name would be almost unpronounceable to you with that crude mechanism for making the noises you call language, but you can call me Topsy. If you're feeling formal, I also answer to Doctor Topsy. It's an inside joke, but hopefully we clear that up later. Speaking of jokes, I've often said that when he made humans, the all-knowing god must have been admitting a mistake with his first crew of companions and servants, so he dumbed down your design a bit. Thus, you having such difficulty pronouncing what I consider a perfectly commonplace name. Still, it comes in handy, as it keeps me from getting summoned by every Anton, Aleister, and Harry who bumbles his way to the chapter on summoning in whatever book on the dark arts is in his possession.

As a demon, I *am* the black arts, and don't like to be interrupted by amateurs, thank you very kindly.

Which of course begs the question, why am I speaking to you? Well because, frankly, I suspect your friends and family think you to be a fool. Oh please, do not be offended. I don't mean that in a drooling imbecile sort of way. Frankly, those people have neither imagination nor intellect to understand what I have to say. I mean it more in a "Head always in the clouds, heart always in a book", dreamer sort of way.

Everyone needs somebody to talk to, after all. It makes all of us, even demons, feel a little better, don't you think? A shoulder to cry on, a friendly ear, the reason bartenders stay employed? I think I've an accurate idea of you. A little bit look-I've-just-bought-a-Lovecraft-shirt with a smidgeon of Lord of the Rings thrown in? Of course you are. No use in denying it; nothing to be ashamed of, anyway. And you make the perfect confidante, for who will believe you about me, should you be inclined to blab? Perfect.

I think that we get bad press. I know, we're *demons*; what kind of press do we expect? Maybe not bad press as much as unfair. We aren't running around tempting mortals for their souls, and tearing apart victims in all kinds of icky bloody tortures once we've lured them into our grasps! Well, not as often as we used to. Well, a bit, alright I grant, it does come up, but it isn't the overwhelming obsession like your films and books make it out to be.

Prove it, you say? Well first off, I would point out that here I am, talking to you! You haven't been whisked around straight to hell, have you? You still have all of your appendages still attached do you not? Please, go do an inventory yourself if you don't believe me, I'll wait... I did not do a thing to *that*! That *is* the correct size, and I had nothing to do with the present situation. Don't think you can sucker me into some major corrective surgery for what God neglected that easily!

We have many more diverse interests than that. I could prove it with a couple of stories of my recent fun. Then, maybe you'd see it wasn't all just rending flesh and dastardly drawn up contracts. Why, yes! I could give you a contrast and compare! I could give you two stories, one that is maybe a little more, shall we say, true to our reputation. The other could be, the kind of thing I *really* enjoy, and I could leave it to you, my new friend, to decide which one was the most, shall we say, demonic?

So what shall it be first? Blood on the walls? Or the kind of evil which warps the soul?

~/~

Why did I know you were going to go for the bloody one? Predictable, really. Nothing you people seem to like more than seeing one of your own's blood and viscera flying everywhere. I wonder why you even bother with music. Put out a song and call it, "Screams Of The Tortured Dying". It would probably sell a million copies. Oh well, I'm nothing if not obliging.

It all started simply enough. I was in my study, you know, studying things--what do you mean 'what things'? Alright, if you must know, I was thumbing through some old Chick Publications comics. I can't help myself; I find those things hilarious. The guy was a special talent, I can tell you that, worth his weight in ichor to us.

Anyway, I was giggling away, when I heard my name spoken on the mortal plane. Most demons can hear if a mortal speaks their name. Of course, your more powerful demons hire lesser infernal folk to hear their name for them. Baphomet would never get anything done if he heard his name every time it was invoked. He keeps an imp handy almost like an answering machine, who goes through the daily mentions, weeding out the casual oaths. I've thought about getting one, but really, my name is so difficult to pronounce, it doesn't seem worth it. When somebody manages to vomit out my name, I want to see what they're about for myself.

Upon hearing my name, I raced to its source and found an area to make my appearance nearby. I entered into the world in a countryside. You don't appear right away next to the speaker; that's bad form. Instead, you try to find an unobtrusive spot near them. It's a shock to see someone just step out of the ether, and it leads to questions. Yes, we have gone for the big appearances for shock and awe, but to be honest, half the time we just use flashpots like any magician. It's cheaper. No, you want a look at the little scoundrel taking your name in vain, it's better to see the situation and plan what you want to do rather than going in tail half-cocked. That and when we manifest, well it's embarrassing, but there's always a little brimstone. Can't be helped.

Peering out from my hiding spot in the nearby woods, the situation became apparent. What I spied with my evil eye was a middle-aged, overweight man standing next to a relatively nice Mercedes. His face was flushed, his brow tensed in annoyance. In one hand was the mutant hunk of metal that made up part of the Mercedes-Benz jack, his other he was shaking as if injured, and he was yelling forcefully enough to cause a spray of spittle to fly with every eruption of his jowly mouth.

Now, I knew the situation. Someone didn't know how to change a flat on his own car. Perfect! He'd accept any help offered with no second thoughts! A bit of checking my internal GPS gave me an idea of where I was: somewhere in New York State, close enough to the Hudson Valley to give me my cover story! Stepping back to my personal chambers, I grabbed a few things I thought I'd need and slammed them into a svelte designer bag before putting on a glamor for appearances. Slinging a camera around my neck, I popped back where I had been just a moment before.

"Hello?" I called out, stepping near to the edge of brush.

The man lunged backwards, startled, "Oh! Hello! You gave me quite a fright!"

"I'm dreadfully sorry," I said stepping out into the road, "I heard someone, well, cursing. I was in the area taking photos, and frankly getting myself turned around, so I thought I'd see if I could help. Maybe figure out where I am."

"If you can figure out this blasted jack, you'd be saving my tuchus!" the man said with a beaming grin. "Sorry if you heard me, but I assure you, I wasn't cursing." He smiled again and wiped his brow, "A habit I picked up as a child, when I'm especially angry I just make up a word and bark it loudly. Hopefully, god can forgive me that!"

He certainly could, but I am not in the forgiving business. The opposite, really. Transgressions, even those of an accidental nature such as this, must have consequences. There is no point to having rules if one is not prepared to dish out the punishment which comes with breaking them. I mean that for humans, of course. I break any rule I find inconvenient. I suppose if I found punishing a mortal for speaking my name inconvenient, I could break that one too, but when is that ever going to happen? Oh no, no fun for me please, all full up here?

I chuckled aloud, and said, "Here's to hoping he doesn't consider intent. Let me take a look at it. Maybe I can save you considerable blast and bother!"

"You do, and I owe you a drink and a meal and a ride back to wherever you got turned around from!" he said with a broad smile on his broad and sweating face.

I had no problem with the jack. It was a Mercedes after all. My tribe had quite a lot to do with their original designs, as it were. Good German engineering. It's a shame we couldn't figure out a way to let the nutter win that war. But the angels got sick of us fixing up his tactical errors and stepped in to counter us. Goody-two-shoes spoiled sports! Oh well, his loss gave people hope back I suppose, and hope is where damnation is truly made and fermented, after all.

He watched me carefully while I worked. You could tell the man had an inquisitive nature. He wasn't just standing by while some chap labored for him. He was paying attention, learning as he went so he would never be in such straits ever again. I hadn't the heart to tell him he wouldn't.

"Well, thank goodness for that! I'd have been here all the live long day if you hadn't come along!" he said, clapping me enthusiastically on the shoulder once I had let the car down.

I turned to look at him, smiling with what for all

the world was the smile of a good Samaritan happy in a job well done. He thrust out his hand, "Doctor Richard Farnsworth. Pleased to meet you, sir! And your name is?"

"What a happy coincidence! I'm a Doctor as well, Doctor Topsy, Seth Topsy!" I said while vigorously pumping his extended hand.

"Well, Seth! I do believe I owe you at least a drink, but I'd be delighted if you'd dine with me at my house tonight! I don't get many guests, to be honest. Where are you parked?" The words came in a nervous, yet relieved, rush.

"I'll tell you what," I replied, "if you can give me your address, it'll give me a chance to clean up a bit first."

He wrote his address on the back of a business card, which I noted was a very nice stoneware linen with thermographed type. Very classy. We arranged that we should meet at his house later that very night. I took note of the address as he drove off. He wasn't just any type of doctor, apparently. One needed a wealthy clientele to afford such an elegant spot in the old space-time.

~/~

A vanish here, a reappearance there, and I was driving off to the good Doctor's mansion in the woods. I had on a nice enough suit, nice, but not too nice. I was playing the part of a general practitioner, after all. In these 1960's America, your Doctor would be upper middle class, but not filthy with it. I also wanted to establish myself in the inferior position. I needed him to be trusting of me, and the great and mighty always tend to trust the slightly less successful members of their trade so long as they act like they are content with their lot in life. A corporate lawyer loves the guy playing local yokel lawyer adjudicating chicken cases. They tend to assume there is some special honor in "not doing it for the money". To complete my appearance of subservience, I was driving a very nice Oldsmobile, upper middle class all the way.

I made a point of bringing a special wine and showing up ten minutes early. Early always shows throat like a dog rolling over and baring its neck to the wolf. He greeted me at the door of his estate himself, which was a surprising gesture, one he explained away, saying, "I only hire servants for special occasions and cleaning, really. I believe a man should know how to cook and take care of himself, without a woman's help, if need be. Anyway, how often do you even have guests out here in the sticks?"

His explanation told me plenty. Firstly, I did not count as a "special occasion". This was fine with me, as I didn't want to be one, and being so would complicate my plans for the evening. Secondly, he told me in no uncertain terms that this was a second home, judging by his wedding ring and the lack of a wife, who I assumed was staying in the city and not, as he put it, "out in the sticks". But most importantly he told me we'd be alone tonight, just the two of us.

He asked if I minded dining in his study instead of the dining room, explaining the latter was too large for comfort. I happily agreed. A quiet study, two chums dining casually, a perfect situation. Sure enough, when we entered there was a nice, smaller table away from the fireplace perfect for informal dining. We settled in, and he served. After swallowing a mouthful I asked, "This is absolutely delicious! You made this yourself?"

"It's good enough I suppose, but truthfully, half of cooking is just following directions. But I thank you for saying it," Farnsworth said, waving his fork as he spoke. "You said you were a Doctor?"

I decided to take the conversational gambit. "Oh, yes. Nothing glamorous enough to afford the likes of this. Just a small practice in the suburbs." All of this I said in a self-deprecating tone Farnsworth devoured along with his meal.

"Oh, there is nothing wrong with that!" he declared. "For every single person saved by the likes of me, there must be a hundred who come to you for help."

"Kind of you to say," I smiled.

We conversed quite freely after that. I gave him the manufactured details of my imaginary practice, and he gave me of his in kind. It turned out the good doctor was a surgeon and nerve specialist. He was very expensive, a fact he only half-downplayed, eager as he was for more of my fawning, which I gave. During a lull in our conversation, I feigned a need for a bathroom break so I could do some quick off dimensional sleuthing about the man. By the time I returned, I had a full understanding of Doctor Richard Farnsworth, and my plan was complete in my mind. I'd had a seed of an idea before, but now it was blossoming before my eyes. My wine would have a splendorous effect upon him, being as I had made sure it was at least part ichor.

Ichor should be explained, I suppose. It is the blood of the gods. At least that was the original recipe, but much like plasma for you, my kind has been manufacturing it on our own since forever. What are gods? Well, you could run through your various mythos and come up with dozens of different answers, and all of them would be more or less correct. Suffice it to say that, since the creator stopped talking to anybody and everybody, the role of god has been filled by various individuals from the demon and the angel variety. The best of the best, as it were, or you could say the one's with the biggest egos. I mean, if you were petty. I would never say that, of course, at least not until I was sure of who was listening. Anyway, it turned out that the blood of those A-Grade holy of holies had various abilities in the hands of the mystically inclined. The more mystic, the more abilities. As a demon myself, you don't really get much more mystic, do you? With a few words here and a wave of your hand there, you can make it do all kinds of things. It will heal just about any wound, knit up your skin and muscles just like nothing happened. It can also do some other things.

Like what it did to my host right then.

I heard a shocked gasp escape him. His hand released the glass he had been drinking from with my fine vintage in it. I sighed at wasting even a little ichor as it crashed to the floor beneath his seat.

I tchhed, "Such a shame, you know that particular vintage is absolutely impossible to get around here." I smiled my most winning evil smile as I stepped towards the man. "It has amazing properties, don't you think? There you are, unable to move a muscle, yet completely aware. And here is the really fun part: no matter how much pain I cause you, no checking out with a convenient heart attack for

you! No, you're going to survive all of it, and you are
going to feel all of it! It will be an experience, and
make no mistake!"

I could see the shock and question in his eyes, or
maybe I only imagined I did. "Your little habit of
making up little curses has gotten you into quite a
spot of bother, Doctor Farnsworth! Did you know
that a demon hears its name when it is spoken by a
mortal? We can be quite peevish about the whole
thing, really! Your habit of hiding your cursing has
cursed you very well indeed. Now, where do you keep
your tools of your trade? I'm sure you have a private
office for those off-the-books procedures nobody
likes to talk about. Oh, don't be so coy about it,
Farnsworth. You know the ones, the kind which
come in the middle of the night and leave your
pocketbook flush by morning. Well, no matter, I'm
sure I can find it myself. You're indisposed at the
moment!"

It didn't take long to find what I needed, and I
returned in a trice. "Goodness me!" I said with the
happy smile of a child who had just been gifted a
balloon. "You did have all *kinds* of goodies in your
operating theatre. If only I had more time, but I have
something specific in mind, and one mustn't get
distracted from the task at hand!"

I lifted up the fat doctor as though he were a rag
doll and placed him on his back on the dinner table. I
showed him the scalpel I had acquired for the
evening's entertainment. His eyes didn't grow wide,
they couldn't, but I could see the terror there anyway.
A good demon always knows these things, after all.
You need to not look at the eye because even the
shape of it can lie to you. No, you need to see beyond

the pools of the iris to the depths below, to a place which exists outside of the material plane, for it is in the eye you may catch glimpse of the higher self, the so-called soul. The soul is bare of artifice and cannot hide its terror, and the pureness of its emotions are ambrosia.

I removed his shirt and his thin undershirt, exposing the lily-white flab of his torso. His skin pimpled reflexively at the cool air striking it. I slapped at his tubby belly and watched it wiggle a bit as a bright red hand print appeared on it. "Good thing we're not trying to cut through all that eh?" I grinned at him.

Next, I took the scalpel firmly hand and began. The first cut occurred on the chest, at a diagonal angle near the breastbone. Next, I cut in a long line going up past the shoulder and another at the other end, like a large 'I'. I would take breaks as I cut, so I could watch the man's eyes. It was joyful to see the torment, trapped in there, unable to allow itself the release of screaming. After the first cut, I made a point of picking his head up from the table a little to show him my handiwork. A consummate professional like him would appreciate the view I thought.

"I wonder if you can even guess what I intend to do? Don't you worry, I won't spoil the surprise! But you know, I think using this professional little blade is spoiling some of the fun, don't you? " I said the scalpel on the table next to his ear, so he could hear it clink on the table. I held up a serrated steak knife so he could see it, "I think you'll *really* be able to feel this, don't you think?"

Moving some of the fat out of the way, I could get to work. It was tough going, but I loved every minute of it as I sawed cross ways through the muscles of the pectoralis major. Every screaming pain it caused as one after another of the fibrous muscles of the chest fell to the onslaught of the blade's rasping touch. But good things don't last forever, no matter how much we're enjoying ourselves. Time flies, and all that. It was with a forlorn sigh that I pulled the muscle up and let it flop over the Farnsworth's shoulder.

"Moving on," I said, sing-song. I smiled at the good doctor, drinking in his beautiful agony, his soul and his brain screaming so loudly it was almost audible to the naked ear. "I'd have let that go on a bit longer, Richard, but you're out of shape. I only had so much muscle to work with. I think we can make this next bit of fun last a little longer if we...use something a bit duller?"

I picked up a butter knife and waved it under his eyes, "A good thing you had a full complement of cutlery at the table, isn't it? I might have rushed all of this and just used the scalpel, and what a shame it would have been to cut short our time together."

I moved some more fat and I saw my goal. A happy little M for Misery there in the armpit, if that's how you chose to look at things. Now, an amateur would cut those where it's the most obvious, wouldn't he? But I, my friend, am not an amateur. I am a doctor, after all; that wasn't mere deception.

I began to draw the butter knife with its tiny serrations across the medial nerve cord. The nerves: the delivery system of so many vital sensations and commands to the brain. Like pain. I had to hold the slippery thing taut with two fingers gripping it vice-like as I worked. There was an audible snap as it finally gave way. I did regret that some, it probably would have been much more torturous for him to feel the last shreds of it slowly hacked away, but alas, you can only work with the materials you have at hand.

Next to go was the lateral cord. I humored myself for a moment, as I pulled it tight, flicking it with my finger to hear the musical note it would produce. It might not be high art, but it was music to my ears, and we all play our instruments for ourselves, do we not?

I spared my victim another glance. I could scarcely credit it, but there were beads of sweat on the man's puffy face. The pain must have been beyond human description that even with the ichor steadying his vital signs and keeping him from shock or acute myocardial infarction, his body was still producing a sheen of sweat. I smiled again.

"Well, now that we've gotten those two fellows out of the way, we can get a good crack at the posterior cord!"

The pleading and begging in his eyes I saw then, I savor it on nights when I'm bored and despondent.

Finally, it was over. It didn't have to be, to be sure, for there are plenty of other nerves to play with, but it's no good having a plan if you don't intend to keep to it, now is it? I had intended to wipe out the nerves leading to his surgery arm, and I had. Anything else would be overkill and lacking panache

"I'm going to leave you in a bit, Richard."

I could see a twitch in his eyes.

"Oh, don't worry, I'll be putting you back together. Well, except for the nerves that is. In fact, you will never, ever, ever be able to speak of this to anyone. But I think it's time for you to go to sleep. I wouldn't want you to actually experience the relief of the end of your torment after all."

I waved a hand in front of his eyes and let his consciousness drift away. It did not take long to reattach his muscles and close up his skin. Ichor is indeed magical stuff, after all. All I really needed to do was to hold the muscles down and dab it with the stuff to get the bits and pieces to return to their previous, un-ravaged form. But not his nerves; those I left severed.

I was brisk after that. I carried my charge up to his bed and changed him into his pyjamas. I tsked at him a bit for his taste in bedclothes, but it wasn't worth waking him to say. Instead, I just tucked him up nice and snug in his bed. I cleaned up any trace of my visit: the blood on the table, my plates. I pocketed the wine. Before I left I made sure to leave his plates, and the wine he had opened for us before that. I left it empty, of course, drinking it down in just a few mighty droughts. I was setting a scene.

The scene I set that early sixties night? A middle-aged, rich surgeon, with the country house to himself without the wife. He goes to bed after drinking far, far too much wine. When he wakes, he has no feeling nor functionality in his right arm at all. The diagnosis considering his weight would be a snap judgment. A stroke. Most of the tests would say it was one and given him admitting that he had had bad dreams of some kind all that night would go a long way to confirm it. They would put him on medication, he would never have another stroke, a success of modern medicine!

That was fun, wasn't it? A body torn apart, pain and misery so excruciating it would make a man insane! Funnily enough, the phantom memory lurking in Doctor Farnsworth's memory did indeed drive him mad soon enough. He died in an asylum. So that's one way to do evil's work.

~/~

The next story isn't nearly as fun, I'll admit, but it's quicker. In the 1980s I went to college at Harvard. What could they have to teach me? Not a thing! I had contributed to much of the older texts, after all. But I needed to be in position. Great things were happening in human history, and somebody needed to be nearby to observe and perhaps influence.

So, I became happy normal med student, Neil Topsy. It was fun, I had to admit: no responsibilities, no worries, just basically showing up for classes whose topics I knew intimately. I don't think I so much as cracked a book until we got to some of the newest cutting-edge procedures. This gave me plenty of time to hang about and corrupt the morals of a few law students, most of which would go into politics, of course. I was mainly laying down a back story and making the types of friendships I would need later.

My classmates and I went into the workforce after school. I didn't really keep in touch with most of my former "frat brothers". The things they intended to do with their lives were no more interesting to me than what I was pretending to do with mine. Investment bankers seem to come out of the womb corrupted, and since my little nudges down the path of Gordon Gecko had been easy and fast, they were well on their way to making god knows how many people miserable. Even more so for the lawyers.

One day I was having lunch with my friend Kevin. Kevin was in electronics. He had seen the original home computers, farcical though they were, and had glimpsed the future. Even at this early date, it was becoming apparent he'd been right. They were getting faster and more capable all the time. This thing called the internet he had spoken of so rapturously would soon be coming to homes everywhere.

He was still broke, though, since he worked for a startup, and so I was paying for lunch.

"OK, spill. We've already got entrees ordered, and you've barely spoken," I said to him as we waited. "Come on, if you can't trust me, who can you trust? What's got your head in a cloud?"

"Oh, it's just a marketing issue. We need to find a way to make our company stand out," he said with a shrug.

"Stand out how?"

This got a big sigh from Kevin and a sip of his Coke, a sure sign of cogitation from him. "Well, when we started, we thought we'd be ahead of everybody offering web based emails. You know, a site you could go to to house your emails rather than using the inbox built into your internet service. But now it seems as if everybody and his brother are going to have one unveiling soon. News stories and email all in one, just like ours."

"So it runs on its own web page, and you, what, sign in to view your emails?" I asked sincerely.

"Yeah, but it looks like there's going to be at least five competitors rolling out this year with a similar model. We don't want to get lost in the shuffle. My boss has hinted that the one who comes up with a good idea to make us stand out is probably going to be a really rich guy after we go public," he said, sullenly swishing his ice cubes around in the glass.

I gave him my most charming pal smile and said, "Tell you what, give me dinner to think about it? Hey, two heads are better than one, after all. If I come up with an idea, it's yours gratis. You're the one who bought us all that Jolt for finals the one year, and that stuff wasn't easy to get back then, I figure I owe you at least an idea."

"You come up with one, dinner is on me," he replied.

We ate our dinner and caught up with how we were both doing. We had the same lives of most newly professional people: working hard, not making enough money, but with a sight of it on the horizon soon, et cetera. Neither of us were dating anyone seriously for the same reasons, which was no free time.

When the check came I made to pick it up. Kevin grinned at me and said, "So, no great idea, huh?"

I acted surprised for a second, and then said, "Oh yeah! I had one, nearly forgot! How about giving people groups? You know, for common interests or professions, and stuff. Like a room you host where people can come on your site to talk. It would help with doctors, for sure, but other people could discuss the things they like, like football, or old movies, or stuff?"

Kevin sat back, a stunned look on his face as he scratched his chin. He still said nothing as he leant forward and swirled his ice cubes around a bit. Finally, a radiant smile crossed his face, and he reached for the check.

"Dinner is on me."

And so we parted that night, he with his grand money-making idea, and me with the warm feeling of having done evil's grand work.

$$\sim / \sim$$

I can hear you scream at this page now, "That's it? You gave some computer wonk the idea for message boards????"

Please, hear me out.

The crippling of Doctor Richard Farnsworth might have cost a hundred, maybe a hundred and fifty people their lives due to being deprived of his surgical genius. It certainly cost him his. But past that, what did I do but create a great story to pass around in one of the various bars in Hell when I've been in my cups. Sure, it's funny and all, but still.

Do you really understand how much evil has been done by message boards? Within the year, Kevin's page was up and running at full force, and faster than that, political boards sprung up. People cursed each other and lied to each other every day. Physical threats were made by people named "Plumlover2000".

But it got better yet. Soon, there were web pages dedicated to lying! People began to distrust the old truth tellers in favor of lies they wanted to believe! Soon whole sites became dedicated to just people talking and lying to one another. Wars were fomented there, hate groups exploded as those lonely souls discovered they were not alone, and they began to recruit more to their sides. Murders happened, rapes, all kinds of splendorous things.

Some of my best work.

You see, my dears, this is what we demons *really* want to do. We don't want to torture you. Well, we do, but we're smart enough to know that is only a fleeting pleasure. What we really want to do, is let you create something you're proud of, we want it to be the best you can make or think of, and then, we want to convince you to screw it up for yourselves.

You split the atom, one of us haphazardly mentions it's destructive force.

You create cars, we suggest tanks.

You create movable type, we suggest tabloids.

Now that's good clean fun, right there.

I got a commendation and a medal for internet groups. I can't wait for the next great and wonderful idea you have. There may be a demon among you right now, just itching to give you a suggestion on how you might improve it.

Tea With Anubis @ 3:00

L. Joseph Shosty

11:00 a.m.

The harassment began as soon as church let out. No sooner had the preacher summed up his sermon on "Love Thy Neighbor, Or Else" than Thomas J smote Herbert's arm like it was Gamorra itself. At ten years old, Herbert's body was as yet unaccustomed to pain. The slightest twinge made his muscles freeze in place, and a punch from Thomas J felt like Christ's own ordeal. As he went down on one knee, wailing, he looked skyward and wondered why God hath forsaken him in his time of suffering.

It being Sunday, Herbert was forced to leave a message with St. Peter.

"How d'ya like that, faggot?" Thomas J crowed.

"Watch your mouth, Thomas J," Momma said, and Daddy followed her warning with a vengeful stare. Never mind that Herbert was in mortal agony, or that he hadn't done anything to warrant the attack.

"Now get in the car, both of you," Daddy said, "and I don't wanna hear a peep until we get home."

11:12 a.m.

Slorp.

Thump.

Wiggle-wiggle.

This was the sound of a chicken wiggle, a particularly disgusting form of torture Thomas J often administered when he had run out of ideas. Making his kid brother's life hell was an important concern for him, and chicken wiggles kept Herbert firmly in distress until Thomas J could pull a new form of suffering from the de Sadian manifesto he called a brain. A chicken wiggle involved wetting his finger with saliva (slorp), stinging Herbert's tender ears with a series of thumps (thump), and then shoving his slimy finger into Herbert's ear canal and wiggling it back and forth. It was a heinous crime, and would be tantamount to the death penalty should anyone ever die as a result.

"How d'ya like that, faggot?"

Herbert had been contentedly munching on a blueberry muffin when the assault occurred and continued to do so. A younger brother had two choices when being picked on by a sibling. He could either scream bloody murder in hopes of annoying his parents so much they would punish both his older brother and him for horsing around, or he could stoically continue his life as though suffering were part of existence. He chose the Buddhist approach. Daddy was driving, and Momma was checking her makeup in the passenger side mirror. Either could see what was going on, and if they wanted to punish Thomas J they had ample visual evidence.

"You must be a girl if you like havin' things shoved into ya! Haw!"

Herbert began to hum a Negro spiritual.

12:02 p.m.

As the car pulled into the driveway, Thomas J slapped the half-eaten muffin from Herbert's hand. It was the snake-quickest thing Herbert had ever seen. One moment he was enjoying wholesome blueberry goodness, and the next Thomas J's was whipping it from his grasp and sending it careening off the seat and into the floorboard. Herbert blinked once before Thomas J shot back to his side of the backseat, where he began pointing and laughing.

"Haw! You stupid idiot!" he roared. "You can't hold on to nothin'!"

Herbert was still shocked and stared at where the muffin lay in the floorboard when Daddy turned his head around like a wrathful owl. "What the hell is goin' on back there?"

"The stupid faggot dropped his muffin."

Momma: "Thomas J!"

"He slapped it out of my hand," Herbert protested.

"Well get the damned thing off the floor before ants get to it," Daddy roared. "That's what you get for eating in front of your brother. He ain't got nothin' for himself."

Doesn't have anything, Herbert wanted to say, but all correcting Daddy's grammar would do was get him in more trouble. He obeyed and picked up every crumb. Thomas J grinned crookedly at his handiwork.

12:15 p.m.

Momma and Daddy were in the house having Sunday Sex as they often did after church. Out of respect Herbert sat on the front porch and watched the birds. Thomas J was there out of a lack of having anything better to do. He was watching Momma and Daddy as best he could between the blinds.

"He's playin' with her tits, Herbie," he whispered. "Git it, Daddy, git it."

"Why don't you come away from the window, Thomas J? That's disgusting."

"'Cause when it comes time for me ta screw a girl I wanna know what I'm doin'. I don't wanna be like you. You ain't gonna never know what to do with your pecker except pee."

Daddy began to grunt like an animal, and the bedpost knocked against the windowpane. Thomas J started whispering "Yeah! Yeah! Yeah!" as though he were participating. Herbert watched a killdeer bathe itself in the concrete birdbath beneath their old pine tree and tried to tune out Sunday Sex, but to no avail. Abruptly the knocking stopped. Dad groaned, Momma sighed, and Thomas J made a noise that reminded Herbert of someone being choked.

"Uh, okay," Thomas J said. "Well, uh, yeah. Uh, uh-huh. That--that was pretty informative. Uh, yeah."

The killdeer finished bathing and was hopping along the ground. Herbert watched it venture into the neighbor's yard, wishing he could go there, too.

To stay.

1:02 p.m.

After Momma and Daddy had finished Sunday Sex and had cleaned up, Daddy got a beer and went to watch the game while Momma fixed a late lunch. Herbert sat at the kitchen table with his pen and paper jotting down ideas categorized not on worth but on financial feasibility. It was his opinion that an idea was only good if one had the money to put it to use. Thus he had put his theoretical specs for a faster-than-light propulsion drive at the bottom of the stack and a recipe for homemade napalm on top. He wrote:

Two parts laundry detergent to one part gasoline. After thorough testing I've discovered that certain properties within the gasoline interact with the detergent to form a sort of gelatinous substance much like the napalm used on our enemies during the Vietnam Conflict. If ignited it would work in a way quite similar to the genuine article. Using a special chemical I developed with the chemistry set I got last Christmas, it is no longer necessary to let the mixture sit for several days before it is ready for use.

The paper jerked under his hand, and the pen went sliding across the page, leaving an ugly black streak. Herbert glared at the culprit. Thomas J guffawed and sprayed bits of half-eaten banana everywhere.

"Haw [smeck]! How d'ya like that, faggot?"

"Don't you have anything better to do than sitting around here bugging me?" Herbert asked.

Thomas J stuck a finger up his nose and liberated the ghastliest booger in Creation. He wiped it on Herbert's sleeve.

"Nope."

Without another word Herbert went upstairs to change.

1:06 p.m.

Upon entering his room Herbert found his poster of Albert Einstein had been given a penis and testicles courtesy of Marks-a-Lot and Thomas J. There were marbles ill-concealed beneath the blankets of his bed. His slippers were filled with shaving cream. Herbert sighed, wondering where Thomas J found the time, and what would happen if his brother ever turned his energy toward more constructive pursuits. Like snipe hunting, for instance.

After changing into his Yoda t-shirt Herbert was met at the kitchen doorway with vilest chicken wiggle in recorded history. Herbert wasn't sure, but there was at least a fifty-fifty chance the very finger that was shoved into his ear was the same one that had wiped a booger on his sleeve. The thought of it made him jerk away, and though he was ten and scrawny and Thomas J was thirteen and built like a moose, Herbert shoved his brother with all his might.

"Imbecile!" he shouted, but his hands bounced harmlessly off Thomas J's burgeoning muscles.

Satan's own grin spread across Thomas J's face. "Yer dead, faggot," he growled, and dropped Herbert with a punch to the gut. A shockwave ripped through the boy, the world turned inside out, and the next thing Herbert knew he lay face down on the floor. He felt himself being flipped over, and Thomas J perched on Herbert's chest like a brawny vulture.

"Well, now," Thomas J hissed, "You think you're tough, Herbie? You can just consider your ass kicked from here on. You think I'm playin'? Just watch this." Herbert watched wide-eyed and impotent as the frozen turkeys Thomas J called hands moved within inches of his face. What would he do? What would Thomas J do that meant touching his face, he thought? Herbert cursed his ten-year-old body. Why couldn't he fight back right? And where were

Momma and Daddy? Why couldn't they hear, couldn't see, what was going on?

Thomas J's thumbs brushed Herbert's eyelids...

"Boys! Lunch!" Momma shouted. Thomas J hesitated. There came the belated, metallic screech and thump as Daddy moved his La-Z-Boy upright and stood. Thomas J slipped off Herbert and smacked him in the head once to let him know this wasn't over. Herbert knew it wasn't.

"Herbie, what the hell are you doing on the floor?" Daddy didn't wait for a reply. "I said get off the floor."

Herbert said nothing, but instead pulled himself up and looked for Thomas J. His brother was already at the table eating the cold cut sandwiches Momma had prepared. His face was carefully averted from Daddy and Herbert in the hall, but Herbert could see the smirk plastered around the big bites of sandwich. It was further reminder that this was not over, not by a long shot.

1:30 p.m.

There is a moment of absolute mental clarity. The Greeks called it an epiphany, and they probably still call it that, only nobody bothers to study them anymore. In an epiphany a person's mind is so clear that the answers to some, most, or all of their problems become remarkably clear. It is a time when all the neurons and myriad chemical reactions come together in a sort of biological alignment. An eclipse, if you will, of the muddle-headed cloud under which most of us live our lives. In that space, which rarely lasts more than a second, man achieves his ultimate potential for thought. He would know the secret of life if he had presence of mind to ponder it, though few seldom have such ability and can only ponder those problems close at hand. For Herbert, everything that was his family life became clear. His parents, though they might love him, did not like him. They did not understand him or how he could choose to read science books when he could be outside playing football. But they did love and understand Thomas J. He was their kind of people. He talked about people instead of ideas. He played sports, read books only when trapped like a rat in a trap, and was aggressive toward anything beyond his understanding. Like any good person should be, or so his parents said. He had a strong fear of God, too. The worst beating Herbert had ever received came when he admitted to his parents that he wasn't sure there was a God.

Yes, Thomas J was their favorite by a country mile. In their eyes he could do no real wrong. That was why he could get away with picking on Herbert. Their rationale seemed to be that since Herbert was not like the rest of the family he brought such things on himself. Thomas J could cuss like a sailor or steal money like Herbert had seen him do more than once, and all they would do is scold him. Were Herbert to do the same thing, he would be beaten and ostracized, and not even in that order. Thomas J, on the other hand, could get away with anything.

Murder.

The thought hit Herbert like another gut punch from Thomas J. Cold water ran down his spine and turned his bowels to ice. Thomas J could get away with murder. Oh sure, the cops might not like it too much, but Momma and Daddy wouldn't touch a hair on his head. In fact, Thomas J had been about to do something very bad to Herbert in the hall, something to do with his head. Had he planned to kill me then, Herbert thought? The thought would have been as unlikely as frogs doing Shakespeare to another kid his age, but Herbert had seen the smile on Thomas J's face. He was only ten and lacked experience to know those eyes were devoid of humanity, but he knew enough to realize there was something terribly, terribly wrong with his brother.

Thomas J was planning to kill him. Herbert knew that now. He'd probably been planning it since Herbert was in the cradle, but he'd never had an excuse 'til now. Herbert had always been passive, his only actions against Thomas J being the occasional protest when his brother would hurt him. That shove had been his first real act of defiance, and it had set off the black in Thomas J. He couldn't allow this to happen. Preservation instincts kicked in, and Herbert, still standing in the hallway, began to mentally scramble for a solution. He had to get his brother before his brother got him.

That's when his thoughts fell on the sheaf of notes Thomas J lying on the table, the ones Thomas J had caused him to ruin. Herbert gave a small smile, perhaps the first real smile in his life. He had his answer.

1:35 p.m.

He ate lunch with his same small vigor. His bites were passive, slow, methodical. Thomas J smacked his lips and chewed with his mouth open. He talked around half-chewed hunks of bread, and sprayed crumbs when he spoke. Just as always. It was a typical Sunday lunch, down to everyone completely ignoring

Herbert and discussing topics that tended to make them red 'round the neck. Mostly, though, Momma and Daddy commented on Thomas J's antics.

"Have another muffin, son," Daddy said. "Look at that boy eat, June. Look! He's gonna be big." His eyes lit up. "A football player."

Daddy's comment and the Sermon on the Mount vied for importance. It being Texas there was no greater profession than that of football player. It was like the ideal of the priesthood merged with the socially stratified positions of doctor, lawyer, and movie star all rolled into one, though much more exciting than any of the four on a Friday night. Thomas J's position in the family as well became clear, bright, and shining. He was his parents' sole hope for greatness. He was their chance for immortality. Thomas J's future heroics would deify them in the community.

"Here, Thomas J," Momma said, "let me get you another sandwich."

I'd like another sandwich, Herbert thought.

"Growing boy's gotta eat," Daddy supplied.

Herbert supposed he would just wither and shrink. He finished his meal and began to plan.

2:02 p.m.

He gathered what he needed and took it upstairs to his room. Momma would be indisposed for the rest of the day with housework while Daddy would most likely fall asleep in front of the TV. That left the house to Herbert and Thomas J, and the place just wasn't big enough for the both of them.

He rummaged in the garage until he found the device he was looking for, the pressure pump and tin reservoir Herbert had assembled for Momma to spray pesticides when she worked in her garden. It was supposed to have been a gift, but for some reason he'd never given it to her. Now he knew that something greater than himself had stopped him from delivering it, and that the pump's true purpose was waiting for just this moment to reveal itself. He attached a piece of hose to it, and it became a weapon. With duct tape and a flat plastic toy he fashioned a brace at the hose's opening where taped down his father's favorite Zippo, the one with the Rebel Flag. He filled the tin's reservoir with his own mixture of homemade napalm complete with his own special quickening agent, mixed until ready and closed the lid. The rest of the materials he needed he found in his toy box.

2:50 p.m.

Like clockwork, or better yet, God-blessed Providence, Thomas J threw open the bedroom door and sauntered in. Gone was the ugly black glare from before, and in its place was the vacant grin he wore when he was about to get to some serious meanness.

"Hey, faggot, what're you building? Looks like some new semen pump. You gonna stick that hose up your butt and get your fill of gayness every day now instead of just on Wednesdays?"

Herbert ignored him.

"Good," he said, "I'm glad I didn't have to go and find you."

Thomas J looked puzzled. "Whatcha mean, faggot?"

"Thomas J, do you know what a prodigy is?"

"That's one of them stupid computers, ain't it?

Only geeks and faggots play with computers."

Herbert had heard Daddy say the same thing more than once. "No Thomas J, a prodigy is someone who's very good at things. Better, say, than he should be at his age."

"What're you talkin' about, Herbie? You're talkin' all funny. What, you think you're better than me?" Thomas J came back with the black stare and inched closer with his hands in fists.

"Oh, I'm better than you, all right," Herbert replied, testing the tension of a spring one last time. "I'm a prodigy, you know. I'm smarter than everyone in this family put together. I can read words you can't even spell, and understand them. I know Shakespeare, and I can build things scientists can. I can do anything I want to if I put my mind to it. That's why I'm building this, because I can and because I hate you, Thomas J."

His brother rocked back on his heels. "What'chu sayin'?"

"I hate you." There, he said it again. Now, pause to let it sink in. "I've always stood by and let you pick on me, do whatever. You've humiliated me more times than I can count. All I wanted in this family was to be me and to be left alone to do what I chose, but you couldn't let me. You are the one Daddy and Momma love, and you could do whatever you wanted to me so long as they didn't have to hear about it. And you did, didn't you, Thomas J? I've never known peace here. And now you've threatened my life as well." He put tape over the label on the control switch and wrote over it with a Marks-A-Lot.

"What're you talkin' about? I never threatened you. I don't threaten. I do! I do things, I mean, and if

I wanted to kill you I would. I ought to, you bein' a faggot and all."

"I'm not a faggot. Do you even know what that is?"

The pause that followed was too long. "Shut up, you little punk," Thomas J threatened with his bunched up fists. "You're the stupid one. You've always been stupid."

"Think whatever you need to get by," Herbert replied and pumped thirty pounds of pressure into the reservoir.

"What are you gonna do with that?"

"Kill you with it."

"Bullshit," Thomas J sneered. "You ain't got the guts, you little sissy. You cry to Momma every time you stub your toe. You ain't killin' shit."

"Whatever you say, Thomas J, just stand right there." He sighted his brother in on the crosshairs taken from one of his toy guns. "Just hold that pose, and we'll see." He flicked the Zippo, and it lit on the first try. Now that's craftsmanship.

"You know," Thomas J went on hatefully, "you really are stupid. You think this scares me? You think you can scare me with stuff that scares you? You're just a little rat, and when this thing doesn't work I'm gonna beat the shit out of you."

The crosshairs were sighted, the hose was pointed right at him. The Zippo was burning, and there was plenty of pressure in the tank. Herbert picked up his firing mechanism and checked his watch.

2:59:45 p.m.

"Almost time," Herbert said. "I think you'll like

this. Oh, and if it doesn't work you better kill me because if you don't I'll keep trying until I find a way to kill you." He waited until the clock struck 3 p.m., then, in his best action movie super cop voice he said, "How do you like this...faggot?"

He pushed the button clearly marked "Fire".

Carol Mountain

Barrie Darke

Like all slightly mad ideas, it was the product of a hazy, easily-forgotten deductive leap. Boredom at work also came into it. Hendricks had drifted into working as a night-watchman at a midsize plastics factory. Such places, society was given to understand, could be the target of mischievous arsonists who were unaware of the horrors they would unleash: those jet-black clouds could linger for weeks, having rough consequences for years afterwards. Hendricks' nerve-center was a terrible old portakabin with a phone, a kettle, an example of the first wave of portable TVs (black and white, loop aerial, a *dial* to change channels), and not much else. After two days he was sick of the sight of the place. Now he'd been there eighteen months.

The deductive leap involved the phone. The thought was that, once long ago in the evenings, his phone at home would ring with the clamor of social engagements and arrangements. Sometimes, even, women rang and wanted him to go and see them. He had occasionally been prone, he freely admitted, to ringing friends late on, very late on, if he had emotional pressure to relieve. Nowadays there was less of both of those aspects of life. He was single again, had been for a couple of years after the last shouting match, wasn't a million miles away from turning forty, and he had arrived at the point where he believed it a feminist lie that a man needed to change his socks every day. One pair, let it be said, could last the week.

So, all this was a jumble, floating through, bits of it sticking a little, when Hendricks picked up the phone around twelve on a late-spring night, and rang his own home number.

Self-consciousness would've set in before long, crowding out the strangely pleasing image of a drunken passer-by hearing a faint ring coming from an empty house and getting chills over what kind of news this could be. He expected to reach six rings before stopping.

"Thank God," said a woman's voice, picking up after the fifth ring.

"Fuck, sorry—wrong number, sorry to've bothered you," Hendricks gabbled.

"No, don't--I'm glad you rang," he heard the voice say as he took the phone from his ear. He put it back. There was something about the voice, above and beyond it being a woman's and possibly a blonde woman's, that held him. How often was it you heard naked, pleading desperation in another person's voice? You had to go back to schooldays for that. Also, something was insistent that he'd dialed extra carefully to avoid this kind of mishap.

"Can you help me?" she asked.

"Who...Hold on, hold on," he said.

"Can you help, please? I need help."

"Wait, just wait. Listen. There might've been a mistake."

"It doesn't matter, can you --?"

"What number is that?" he cut in, using his authoritative voice. "I know I called you, but I was expecting someone else to answer. So, what number is that?"

"I don't know," she said.

"Well whose house are you in?"

"I think it must be yours. Isn't it yours?"

"Are you...okay, listen." His thoughts threatened to whip away. "Okay, right. What picture's above the fire place?" At some unknown point he'd stood up.

"A picture of Elvis," she said. "Young Elvis, looking nice."

He left a pause. Then he asked, "Who is this? What're you doing there?"

"There isn't time for all that," she told him.

"I bloody well think there is. What are you doing in my, in my fucking gaff?" He had no clue what he'd been watching on TV to come out with a word like "gaff".

"They're coming to get me," she said. "I thought I'd be safe here, but I don't think I am. You have to help me."

"Fuck off. This is a joke," he said. He shook his head, as if she could see him and would snap back to reality in short order.

"You're someone who can help."

"Listen, listen. I'm coming over now. I'm going to have a fucking race with the police to get there. So, you better get going right, fucking, *now*." He hung up. He didn't move.

He didn't drive, he hadn't enough money for a

taxi, the buses had stopped about half an hour before, and his house was an hour's walk away. Still, he would've gone and flailed away if she'd been a man. Since she wasn't, he paced around for a while then sat back down. He considered ringing his next-door neighbor, to see if they wouldn't mind glancing through the window to make sure everything was ticking along nicely, but he didn't know his next-door neighbor's number, or, for that matter, their name. He wondered if this was an elaborate ploy by a plastics factory arsonist, and decided—though it was hard to think straight—it probably wasn't.

After a couple of minutes he picked up the phone again. He was careful in pressing the right buttons. It was answered again after the fifth ring.

"I hoped you'd call back," she said. "I wanted to say sorry, but I didn't know what else to do, I had to go somewhere. I'm sorry."

"Let's just…let me go through this." He forced a calm tone. "Is that all right, to just go through this?"

"It is, but I don't know how much time I've got."

"Well, we'll just have to see, won't we?" This stern tone would've been helped by his voice not shaking so much. "What are you doing in my house, is the first big question."

"I thought it looked safe. That's all."

"You said that before. Safe. What does that mean?"

"I thought it would be a safe haven," she said, in a way that suggested she'd been wrong. "I passed it a few times in the night, and knew it was the one. It's empty at night. Not many houses are. So I thought I should hide away here. Otherwise they would've taken me already."

"Now, wait, just wait a second. You can't just...is this the first night you've been in there?"

"It's the third."

"The fucking *third?* How can it be the fucking *third?*" Hendricks knew he was unobservant when not on duty, the same way the cobbler's children ran barefoot, but surely not to that extent, and definitely not with a woman in the house.

"I'm sorry. But it's true."

"Jesus Christ...why are, who are they; why are you hiding?"

"They're reducers."

"They're what?"

"They're reducers."

"What...what does that mean?"

"I don't know for certain. It won't be good, though."

"Why don't you call the police?"

"The police?" She laughed joylessly. "The police won't last two minutes against this lot. They'll knock them into scarecrows. They'll scare the crows away."

Hendricks sat forward, one hand rubbing his shaved head, which felt very hot and very crammed and engaged in an act of overt betrayal against the rest of him. "Just...explain. I can't ask any more questions. Just explain what I need to know."

"I don't know much myself yet."

"Why are they after you? I'm presuming it's drugs, is it?"

"No. No, it's not that. It's the old story, I suppose. They don't want us to live like we do. What else is it, ever?"

"But what are they going to do? What does 'reducers' mean? I mean, are they going to...hurt you, or…?"

"It'll be worse than just hurting me. I don't want to think about that. I'm safe here, for now."

He was up and pacing again now. He even looked out of the window. "You said before I was someone who could help. Didn't you say that?"

"Yes."

"How, then? How can I help?"

There was a pause. It was more than enough for Hendricks to know what she was going to say.

"I thought you'd know that," she said, her voice a wave.

"How am *I* supposed to know?"

"I just…thought that was the way it works. I'm sorry…"

"You have to tell me what I can do. Think of something, and I'll do it, if I can."

"I don't know what it would be. This has never happened to me before. But there should be someone who can help, who can stop them. I thought it might be you."

"How can --?"

"Oh, no," she moaned. "No."

He could hear her moving, presumably towards the window. "What? What?"

"Oh Jesus," she said, the air stranding the words. "They're outside already. They're in the garden."

"Just…tell them you've got a gun," Hendricks said, his voice rising. "Shout you've got a gun."

"They'll laugh at that," she said, her voice low and rushed.

"There's knives in the kitchen. Get one, hold it up so they can see it."

"They're smoking in the garden. Getting ready, I

suppose. Getting it out of the van. They'll be—"

The line went dead.

As people only ever did in movies, Hendricks stared at the phone before putting it down. He tried ringing again, but this time it wasn't answered. He thought of the passing drunk again, and what chills they would feel now.

~/~

Hendricks was by now the least fit he'd ever been, in a life without much exercise even when he was young and out and about more, but he supposed it was adrenaline which allowed him to run in the short bursts he did. He saw not a single soul on the way there, and couldn't work out if there was something askance about that or not.

When it got too tough to run, he walked as quickly as he could. He tripped often, taking less notice of curbs and so on. At one point he spat, but the spit had bubbling phlegm in it that made it more resilient, so it didn't fly from him but went down his front instead. That was the first time he got angry about all this, though it didn't last long. Mainly he experienced anxiety, similar to that of approaching women in bars, and he didn't want to think what that meant. He couldn't recall a time when he'd been more alert.

Eventually he rounded a corner and saw his house. He could see from a distance that the windows were intact and the door closed. Even the gate was closed, as he'd left it, though this did little to ease his anxiety. He gave an eye to the garden, on his haunches. The streetlight was close enough for him to tell there were no cigarette butts, no footprints in soil. He considered it cowardly to look through the window before entering his own gaff, so he unlocked the door and went in.

It was quiet, dark. He stopped himself calling out "Hello?" There was the sense that the house was empty, undisturbed. The front room, where he had the phone, was in good order, and his Elvis picture hadn't been moved. He checked the phone, and the last number dialed was the portakabin phone. He supposed this shouldn't have given him a chill, but it did.

In the kitchen, the knives were in their drawer. He gave a quick glance around upstairs, then swore and started back to work, running a lot less than he had on the way home. It was still deep in the night time, still no one around. All sorts of catastrophes played themselves out in his head, but everything was fine, the horizon remained unglowing. He'd forgotten to change his splattered shirt, though.

~/~

Hendricks didn't know how, but he managed to wait until the next evening, a rainy midnight, before ringing again. He was nervous, blushing, double-checking that no one was peering in through the black windows. He didn't think it would happen this time; it had been some atmospheric folly opening up in that time period on that one night of the year.

On the fifth ring, she was there. "They're in," was the first thing she said. She seemed to know it was him. Her voice was low. "They're in here. I can hear them."

"Where are you?"

"I'm under the, under the bed."

He wondered--but not excessively--how this could be working, since he had no extension up there and the phone wasn't cordless. "What're they doing?"

"They're moving around downstairs. Setting up the reducer, probably."

"Can't you get out? Jump out of the window, even?"

"Some of them are out there again. Smoking."

"Have they got guns?"

"They're...kind of guns, by the look of them."

"You have to try something. You have to."

"I've tried running. That's it now."

"But you shouldn't be on your own. It's not just you they're after, you said?"

"No, it's not just me, no. There were more of us. We didn't last long. They've got us scattered now. That's how it works for them. They get you separated, isolated. Now they just pick us off."

Hendricks could feel parts of his brain stretching to accommodate this. "Where are they from? Whose authority is this?"

"They have a group authority. They're...they're just the new way of things."

"Can I speak to them?"

"No." Her voice snapped into that.

"I could try, though."

"They wouldn't entertain you for a second. Sorry, that's no reflection on you."

"They're in my fucking house!"

"It's not your house while they're in it, that's the thing. They're doing a job. They're...they're a focused bunch."

"I'll focus them on something," Hendricks said. That phrase hung absurdly in whatever kind of particled air there was between them. When he spoke again his voice was gentler. "What's your name? I don't even know your name."

"Carol. Carol Mountain."

"That's…that's a great name."

"Thank you. It looks good on their reports, anyway. What's yours?"

"Hendricks," he said. "Not with an X, though. Frank Hendricks."

"Well, Frank, nice to speak to you. Shame it couldn't have been in different circumstances."

"I know, I know. It's raining here. Is it raining there?"

"No."

"Right." That was something else to think about later, futilely, he knew. "Listen…I came last night. No one was there. Nothing had been happening, it looked like."

She was quiet for a while. When she spoke again, her voice was also gentle, though in the sense of explaining something to a child. "You spoke to me, though, remember? And you're speaking to me now."

"Sorry," he nodded. He was blushing afresh.

"Oh no," she said. "Oh fuck, no."

"What? What is it?"

"Someone's coming up the stairs. Listen."

There was a rustle as she held the phone out. He could faintly hear someone, a man, calling, "Come on…come down, love…see what we've got for you."

Then another rustle, and she was back, her voice little more than a hiss. "Hear that?"

"I heard it, I heard."

"Oh fucking God, they're at the door."

"Fight them. You fucking fight them. Hurt them all you can."

"There's too many of them, they're too big."

"Claw them. Go for the eyes."

He jumped at the sound of his bedroom door being kicked open, a distorted flat-crack. The voice was still calling for her, come on, love, come out now. Then the line went dead.

Hendricks stayed where he was that night, but he had himself a stormy few hours.

~/~

The next evening, he got up and rang in sick. His boss was unhappy about it, but he had to understand that these things happen to the best of us.

He opted to get drunk that night, to sit up all night and drink until it came to a stop. He had nothing in the house, so he went down to the corner shop and got a liter of whiskey and a liter of vodka. He ate a large meal. He'd stopped keeping up with music, or even giving much time to the collection he'd already amassed, a few years earlier (it seemed to be the sort of interest you maintained when women were around), so he sat and watched TV all night while he drank. It felt stupid, but he paid close attention to the news, both local and national. It felt just as stupid afterwards. He wished he knew another woman; he could get her round, and she could try talking to Carol Mountain. Maybe she would know how to help.

The drinking picked up intensity at 8 o'clock, when he seemed stuck in the midst of soap opera relays. Midnight seemed a bleak continent away, and he took his glass out to the back garden for a while to pace. It was the kind of evening older people called "brisk", so he was back inside before long. No other reason than that.

He couldn't settle, which made him see himself as a fractious child. He'd never known there to be absolutely nothing on TV to hold his attention for a second. It didn't usually bother him what his unknown neighbors thought of him, but he found himself prickly sensitive that evening, wondering if they could hear him walking, if they'd seen him bring the drink in, if they noted through the wall the rapid change of TV channels. He thought he was developing a phobia of being believed insane. Probably there was a term for that. He went to the toilet a hell of a lot.

At 11 o'clock, he stood at the back door for a pitiably long time with the key in his hand. He managed to decide against locking it, but only after that pitiably long time was over. He turned on every light in the place, and opened wide every interior door. The TV was turned off at about half past. A little after that, and in spite of the briskness, the front room windows were opened. Midnight was cloudless, and the moon was half-full. No doubt it had seen worse things than whatever this was.

He drained his glass, took out his mobile, fully charged for the occasion, and rang his number. He stared at the phone as it rang, standing barely two meters away. In his other hand, the kitchen knife he'd had in mind during earlier conversations gave him the artificial courage of an idealistic boy off to enlist.

She answered on the third ring this time, giving

his heart a quiver. He wished, suddenly, completely, almost ashamedly, that he hadn't had a single sip of booze all night.

Her voice was different: thickened, slurred, though whether from drugs or violence he couldn't tell. He got the impression the phone was being held to her head this time.

"I'm glad you rang," she said. "This is to say goodbye."

"Which room are you in?" he asked.

"They've got me in the kitchen," she said.

"I'm here. I'm in the house."

"I can't see anything now, hardly."

"I'm coming through to the kitchen now," he said.

"Just be careful," she said. "I can't help you. You should see the state of me."

"I'm in the kitchen. Where are you?"

"They've got me in front of the sink, but you shouldn't, you should get out."

He stood with his back against the sink, and made slow, almost contemplative swipes with the knife. He covered most angles. "Is that doing anything?" he asked.

"I'm sorry," she said. "They're just laughing at you."

He could hear them: a cruel laughter, as at a child making a fool of itself. He slashed harder, wider. "Am I getting any of them?"

"It doesn't hurt them. Just stop. You might as well." Her voice was even more of a withered thing. "Please stop. This is goodbye."

Hendricks dropped the knife on the floor then kicked it across the room. It vibrated under the washing machine.

"I'm on the fade now," she said. "It doesn't hurt much."

"I'm sorry," he said.

"Thank you, Frank. It's done now. You tried; that's what matters. Thank you. And good luck."

"I'm sorry," he kept repeating, until the line went dead. Then he wandered about the place, drinking until the lights in his head winked out one by one.

~/~

When he woke the next evening, he took up his mobile and held it lightly, airily. Coughing once, he dialed, not thinking beyond the movement of his thumb, and then not beyond the sound he heard in his ear. Of course, when he got to six rings he thought his heart was going to punch itself out of his chest and bounce off the walls. He also thought the gap between the sixth and seventh ring was longer than it should have been. It rang thirteen times before he gave up, though at work, when it reached midnight, he tried again. That time, even his heart seemed to know it wasn't going to work.

At home in the morning, the light flat and a strain on the eyes, he sat down and sent himself a blank email. He looked at it stupidly when it arrived a second later, almost laughed to himself, but he also managed to get up and assemble what he needed to send himself a blank letter. That might be something, he thought.

When it arrived the next day, his own handwriting looking strange and wrong on the envelope. He couldn't be sure there weren't indents on the empty page, no patterns or whorls. He held it up to the window, traced lightly over it with a pencil like they'd done at school on slow afternoons, before concluding there was nothing to see.

He thought of a Ouija board, but somehow didn't have the will. Then one morning, back from work, shaking the rain off his coat, feeling as low and thrashed as he'd ever felt in his life, he soon found himself sitting again on the couch with a pen and a pad of paper. He wrote:

Dear —

You might know who I am. I found myself drawn into this, didn't ask for it, but that's all right. I don't know what's going on, but I want to know what has happened to Carol Mountain. I'm asking you to let her get in touch with me, on the phone or however it's done.

Yours,
Frank Hendricks

It came back the next morning, an hour after he'd gone to bed. The noise didn't usually wake him, but this time his eyes were wide before it even hit the floor. He brought it back to bed with him before opening it. His words were untouched and nothing had been added, but he thought there was something. He held the sheet to his nose. It smelt of strawberries.

On a new sheet, he wrote:

You cowards, doing this to a woman. If you think I can't find you some way, your dreaming. When I do, I'll show you what we do to people who mis-treat women. Look over your shoulder.

Hendricks

Nothing came back the next day. That wasn't unusual for the postal service, but Hendricks couldn't quite see it that way. He kept looking out the window in the evening, and at work that night his boss would've been stunned by his alertness to the slightest sound, stunned and proud.

In the morning he didn't go to bed, but stood by the window, watching for the postman. He had something, just the one letter. When it dropped through the letterbox he could smell the strawberry fragrance before he even picked it up. When he opened it, he saw his words had been crossed out by thick black diagonal lines.

He rang in sick again. His boss was upset, but Hendricks barely noticed. He didn't like using the phone so much these days anyway.

~/~

That night, he kept the retrieved kitchen knife by him the whole time. He had booze in the house, but he actually forgot it was there. It was warmer than it should've been, for the time of day and the time of year, though that could've just been him. On three occasions he heard and briefly saw grey cats bombing around outside, screeching in their babyish, nerve-slitting way. Towards midnight, his music volume seemed to mute and then swell back up, and the phone rang precisely once.

Not long after midnight, a car pulled up near his front door. Its tires had a liquid sound as it stopped, and it shone deep black in the orange streetlights. It looked to be an old design, huge and sturdy. The front doors opened after a few seconds, and his breathing blipped. Two men got out, no one else with them. Hendricks' shoulders dropped, but he soon squared them again. They opened the gate and came up the path without giving the house a look. Nor did they acknowledge him at the window.

There was no knock on the door, but Hendricks went through and opened it anyway. He held the knife in plain sight as he stepped aside and let them in. They passed by without a word, without looking. One of them, he noticed, was carrying a mace: not the spray can, the medieval spiked ball. Hendricks didn't have time to think about that.

"Where is she?" he asked.

The one carrying the mace sat on the couch and put his head back as though resting, though he kept his eyes open. He was either wearing blue lipstick, or he had blue lips. Both of them were shorter than Hendricks by a few inches, but wider, stockier, and more solid. They were wearing new-looking pin-striped suits that were slightly too big. Their skin was mildly tanned, their features thick and blocky and more or less identical, difficult to get a grasp on.

"Where is she?" Hendricks asked again.

"I'm David," the one standing said. He was looking around the room. "This is John." He indicated the other, who didn't look in their direction. "You're Frank?" The voice was a deep brown, deep enough almost to vibrate.

"Just tell me where she is. She spoke to me, there must've been a reason why she could do that. Where is she?"

David went to the phone, picked it up uncertainly. He listened, then put it down, giving a small shrug in John's direction. John had looked round briefly for that.

"What've you done to her? I want to see her."

"It's all right, it's all right," David said. "Shhh. Why don't you shhh now?"

"Fuck that. Let me fucking see her. Now."

"I said shhh."

Hendricks stepped forward, the knife coming up. David unhurriedly took something from his pocket, a flat black rectangle, and pointed it lazily at him. His whole arm felt instantly dug into, clawed through, and the knife fell from his spasming hand.

"All right," David said. "She didn't mean to speak to you. You were a slip-up, that's all. So, it's not important. Not important to anyone."

Hendricks shook his head, but couldn't speak.

"She is…happier now," David went on. "She wasn't happy before, you know. The way she was living, everyone could tell. So, it was up to us to help. There was…a moment of pain, in the reducing, we admit that, but pain is a benefit sometimes. Do you know that? It's true of us, what we do."

"I want to see her," Hendricks managed to say, the pain stealing nearly all of his concentration.

David shook his head. "You wouldn't get anything from seeing her now. You wouldn't. You would prefer not to."

"I want to see her. Just…let me see her."

"Listen. Listen, Carol Mountain wasn't her real name. Did you think it was?" He laughed. "You're not important to her now; she shouldn't be important to you. We advise forgetting this. Forget it, without damage, and you won't have anything like this happen again. We're sure of that."

"I don't want to forget it, though."

John sat forward suddenly and rubbed at the back of his neck with a thick hand.

"You should, because she has forgotten you. She wouldn't know you now." David attempted a smile that was perhaps intended kindly. It didn't work when allied to a low blink rate.

"Well you can take me to her anyway," Hendricks said. "I don't care if she doesn't know me. I know her, and --"

John hiccupped, and a line of clear drool swung slowly to the carpet.

"Take me with you," Hendricks said to David. "I want to go. I want to see her. Please."

He took another step forward, and though it wasn't meant as a threat, David placed a hand on his chest and gave him a shove. Hendricks' feet left the floor, and in a second his back and his head bounced off the wall. He ended up on the floor, the two men rippling in his gaze as they stood over him.

"Forget this," David said. "We can come back here. We can do anything we like here, to anyone. Don't make that your fault."

John had the mace, but he used his fist to punch the wall above Hendricks' head.

"Forget us, and forget her," David said. "She's nothing now. So forget her. Forget her."

They looked at one another, then back down at him. Hendricks stared up at them, but he couldn't say anything, and he couldn't move.

"This won't happen again," David said, and they left.

Hendricks struggled to get up; they were in the car when he made it outside, the engine turning over gently. As far as he could tell, they didn't look back at him. He stood at the gate as they drove slowly away, turning at the bottom of the street. He stayed there, watching, the night pulsing down on him.

Everything and Nothing

Lex Jones

Arthur Vardy stood with hands gripping the steel balcony rail, looking out at the city beyond. It was cold, but that kept the city quiet, especially in comparison to the noise of the party at his back. The event had been in full swing for several hours now. There hadn't been a reason for the party, of course. There rarely was. Just something else to do. And yet even that grew tiresome, hence the extended periods where Arthur would slip away to the balcony. Slip away or blatantly march out there, not that anybody seemed to notice his absence.

"Rather cold out here, isn't it, mate?" said a man in an ill-fitting blue suit as he joined Arthur on the balcony. Arthur always thought that suit made him look like he'd raided his father's wardrobe.

"Just wanted some fresh air, Lance."

"Do you know who half those fuckers are in there?"

"Nope."

"Then why are they here?"

"I ask myself that every time, but it's better than an empty house."

"I'd rather have a couple friends over than a room full of strangers," said Lance. "Honestly, how many of them would you class as friends?"

"Including you?"

"Yeah, go on then. Build your number up a little."

"One."

"It's messed up, mate. You don't need this shit. Tell them all to go home, and you and me can whack out the Xbox like old times."

"Isn't Julie expecting you back?"

"She's out with her friends tonight; mum's got the kids. It's fine, I'm here all night. I just wish we didn't have to share it with these tossers."

"It felt like such a rush to start with, having all these people in my flat, a flat most people would kill to afford, but it just feels pointless."

"Then send them home." Lance patted his friend on the shoulder and drained his beer. "Xbox: hear its calling. I need more booze to keep enduring that shower of shite in there."

Arthur watched as his oldest, and perhaps only, friend made his way back into the party in search of booze. He considered the suggestion to just send everybody home, but the thought of it made him uncomfortable. Yelling for everyone to go, making a scene, it just wasn't him. Better to let them stay until they grew bored and left of their own volition, he decided. Arthur turned back to the cityscape and enjoyed the peace of the night again. It was disturbed a moment later by footsteps, which he at first thought to be Lance come back to try again. But no, Lance didn't wear heels.

"Always on your own, even in a crowd, aren't

you?" The woman who had joined Arthur was slightly smaller than he, even in the heels, with deep red hair and a pale complexion. Her eyes were green but so dark they looked almost black. She wore a dark purple dress with a slit up the side and a low V cut in the front.

"I didn't invite you, Nivian." Arthur sighed.

"Yes you did, you called for me." The woman said with a playful pout.

"I really didn't."

"My sweet boy, you always call for me whether you realize it or not." She stepped closer to him, slinking her arm around his waist. He jumped back at her touch.

"Don't." he said firmly.

"Why the recoil? Are you afraid of me? I *know* you're not repulsed by me." She grinned, pulling herself close to him and walking her fingers up his chin.

"You always turn up when I'm down."

"Of course I do. It's called being here when you need me," Nivian whispered, biting Arthur's bottom lip as he continued trying to ignore her.

"Or you turn up at my lowest to take advantage; that's another way to look at it," Arthur suggested, turning his head slightly to sip his drink.

"Fuck me." Nivian snapped, snatching the glass from Arthur's hand and throwing it against the wall.

"Niv…"

"Here, now. Shut those balcony doors and fuck me as hard as you can."

"There's a room full of people, Niv."

"Oh, who cares, they don't even know you're there!" she laughed. "You've never been afraid to get what you want, we both know that. And once again it's been offered to you on a plate."

Nivian went to the balcony, unfastened her dress and let it drop to the floor, revealing she wore nothing underneath. Her body was porcelain and perfect, exactly as Arthur remembered it. She smiled as she saw his eyes were now fixed on her. She bent herself over the railing, gripping it with her hands and arching her back. Looking back at Arthur over her shoulder she said once more; "Fuck me. Now."

Arthur closed the balcony doors, slipping off his jacket as he went to her.

Ten Years Earlier

Arthur let out a long sigh as he scraped his shoe against a rock, taking away the worst of the excrement. He wasn't even sure what type of animal it belonged to, but the options were numerous, given how far out in the wilderness he seemed to be.

"Note to self," Arthur grumbled out loud. "When someone gives you the vague location of a supposedly haunted house, find out where it is before you set off."

His shoe as clean as it was going to get, Arthur tugged on the straps to his rucksack to tighten them a little, then carried on through the overgrown woodland. After another hour of walking, he came to a clearing. The trees seemed to part in a tall arch, revealing a black-stone mansion in the center of a boggy, brown field. Perhaps once it had been luxurious, the kind of property people in today's world could only dream of owning. But in its current state, it was the furthest thing from welcoming that Arthur had ever seen. Which, he surmised, was probably where the ghost stories came from. A place that didn't need anything resembling tangible evidence to build up such a reputation. Someone would only have to step inside and hear a creaking floorboard, and that would be the end of it.

Arthur was a committed skeptic when it came to ghosts. A part of him existed, however, that clung onto a desperate need to experience something supernatural. A sighting he couldn't explain, a feeling that something was watching him. It was a strange feeling for a skeptic to have; he acknowledged that whenever it was questioned. However, his life had been the sort that was lacking in anything particularly outstanding. Everything had always been 'alright'. Being raised in middle-class England would do that for you. But 'alright' could also be bland, and leave a longing for things that might never be. For some that could manifest in reliance on drugs, drink, gambling. For Arthur, it was a continued desire to visit places which might prove his skepticism wrong.

"They say the guy that lived there before was into demon summoning. And that one of them killed him," Lance had told him. "Nobody's been there since."

Arthur's questions about how a house that size and in such a quiet, remote location would be left untaken by property agencies never got a definitive answer. Questions like that never did where such stories were concerned, which only ever added to the skepticism Arthur felt. He hadn't even been sure the house existed, but the chance to get away from the university crowd for a while had been promising enough to lure him away. Lance was the only one he really got on with; everyone else was a token face in the crowd. He'd offered to come along, of course, but Arthur had relished the chance for some alone time, so made the hike a solitary event. A lone trek to a place that probably didn't exist, that's how he'd seen it. Yet there it was, looming up before him as he entered the clearing.

The door was unlocked, or perhaps too rotten and twisted for the locking mechanism to still work. In either case it opened when Arthur pushed it. The sight beyond was even worse than he'd been anticipating. The door led to an open hallway with a spiral staircase at the back, with church-like windows around the upper landing. Roots had grown through the walls, wrapping around the pillars and staircase. The ground floor had been hard wood, but was now completely sunken and collapsed. A huge hole filled most of the floor, the rest of it sloping down towards it like an open mouth.

Arthur's intention had been to wander about the place. Get some photos, make some notes in his journal. Hopefully see or hear something that might make his search worthwhile. Having seen the state of the mansion now, though, he wasn't sure any of this was feasible. The staircase looked like it might collapse the moment any weight was put on it, so that cut off the upper floors entirely. As for the downstairs areas, navigating safely around the sloping floor and the monstrous hole in the middle was ridiculously unsafe. Better judgement was put aside, though, as Arthur decided he'd come too far now to turn back without even trying to look at the house. The staircase was still ruled out, so Arthur carefully navigated his way around the edge of the room. He could see some doors at the opposite side beyond the hole, so that was where he intended to explore.

"Careful…careful," Arthur instructed himself as he hugged the wall at his back. He moved inch by inch, the wooden floor rotten and moss-covered beneath his feet making it feel like a sheet of ice. His movements were steady, working around the circumference of the room but keeping his gaze fixed on the hole. It wasn't exactly an even shape, stretching closer towards him at some parts than in others, so he daren't take his eyes off it for fear of misjudging his footing.

There was a splash of water from in front of him, down in the hole. His eyes darted to the source of the sound, squinting through the darkness there to try and catch sight of what might be down there. Something large and white moved in the darkness down in the hole, quickly but far too deliberately to be a trick of the light. Arthur startled and slipped, his foot losing its grip as it caught a patch of moss beneath him. He hit the floor awkwardly, then immediately started to slide down the warped ground towards the waiting hole.

"No, no, no!" Arthur yelled, frantically scratching and clawing at the wooden floor to try and gain any kind of purchase. He failed.

Arthur closed his eyes and covered his face as he dropped into the hole, not wanting to see the ground as it reached up to greet him. He felt somewhat relieved when he struck water, his thrashing movements bringing him back to the surface. Coughing and spluttering he waded to the edge of the water, finding it shallow enough there that he could stand, the water reaching just past his waist.

His heart now slowing back down to a

manageable pace, Arthur brushed the wet hair of his fringe away from his face and looked around. He was in a basement, or at least it used to be before it became an indoor pond. Signs or symbols of some kind were painted on the walls, but Arthur couldn't quite make them out in the light. A thought occurred that he might not easily be able to get out of here. He couldn't immediately see any staircase at first glance. To that end he quickly reached into his pocket and fumbled for his phone. Lance had laughed when Arthur bought the military-grade waterproof damage-proof phone case, but it had just paid for itself. At least it would have if the phone were still in his pocket.

"Oh come on, it can't have fallen out, it just can't!" Arthur felt himself starting to panic as he checked one pocket after another.

"Looking for this?" The feminine voice came from behind him. Arthur almost screamed in shock, then spun to see the source. A woman was standing in the water, holding his phone in her open palm. She was naked, had deep red hair, dark eyes and a body that was as pale as it was flawless.

"Who are you? Did you fall down here, too? Are you alright? Your clothes, what…" Arthur rambled this and about half a dozen more questions in a single breath.

"Shhh, I'm fine, everything's fine. I didn't fall down here, I rose up here. A while ago now. I've been so lonely. But now you're here."

"I don't understand."

"My name's Nivian, who are you?"

"Arthur."

"Of course you are; who else would you be?" She

smiled, moving closer to him. Even in the darkness, Arthur could see the water at her waist was barely disturbed as she moved.

"I don't...I think I hit my head. I feel very confused."

"I'm real, I promise." She moved closer still, and he felt her wrap her leg around his beneath the water. His head raced, and his blood travelled undeniably south at her touch. She was beautiful, and beyond. The kind of woman he'd never even seen in real life. She was the stuff of celluloid and wet dreams, and here she was pressing her body close to his. She smelled perfect, which made no sense given the fact she was surrounded by stagnant water.

Nivian pressed her lips against his and kissed him so passionately his head went faint. Arthur's hands found her waist and touched her wet flesh, his heart racing as their skin made contact.

"Tell me what you want." She whispered into his ear, withdrawing from the kiss.

"Erm..." Arthur was suddenly very conscious of his erection pressed against her.

"Oh, you'll get that, that's a given," Nivian said with a smile, her hand reaching down and almost causing Arthur to faint. "No, I mean in life. If you could have anything, what would you have?"

"I don't understand."

"None of this makes sense to you right now, so why should one more question matter?" Niv suggested, her hand working him perfectly. "Just tell me what you want."

"Um...Jesus..." Arthur tried to focus. "Money, I guess. A lot of it."

"Wealth?"

"It just makes stuff easier."

"Done." She nodded, pushing his chest and knocking him back into the water. A second later she was on top of him, and they made love in the shallows.

Arthur's next conscious thought was as he lay in the clearing outside the old house. He had no idea how he'd gotten out of the flooded basement, or whether he'd even made it inside in the first place. At this point it seemed likely that he'd tripped and hit his head, and that everything since had been a dream. His aching groin suggested otherwise, though, as did the fact his clothes and hair were still wet. Getting to his feet, Arthur checked his pocket for his phone and found it there, safely intact and still working. Not only that, but tucked inside was a lottery ticket for that evening's draw. Accompanying this was a card receipt for having purchased the ticket, the details of which showed Arthur's account details. It was entirely legitimate, despite the fact he had no recollection of buying the ticket.

When he arrived home several hours later, Arthur checked the lottery numbers immediately, his jaw dropping wider with every number he read.

Present Day

The apartment always seemed that much larger when he was alone in it, Arthur noted once again. He'd perfected the art of feeling lonely in a crowded room, but at least there were people in the room then. Now he was alone as literally as he was figuratively. His home had all the mod-cons one might expect from something that cost more than most people earn their entire lives: Jacuzzi, flat-screen TV in every room, spacious rooms and expensive art on the walls. None of that made any difference to how Arthur felt when he was alone in it, though.

His company more or less ran itself these days, meaning there was little need for Arthur to go into the office. He could just sit at home and watch the money continue to roll in, perhaps reply to the odd email on his phone, but beyond that his time was his own. With that in mind he'd decided to start writing a memoir, charting his rise from another hopeless student to one of the most successful people on the planet under the age of thirty. He'd leave out the parts about the lady in the flooded basement, of course.

It had seemed so simple, to write about the past decade. Nobody knew it better than he, after all, and his life story was something surely only he could tell. And yet as he stared at the open laptop, he couldn't think of a single word. Well, there was one word that came to mind: Nivian. She was once more filling his thoughts, his loins, every part of him. It was the same cycle, every time. He'd see her, feel like this for weeks, and then the longing and desperation for her would be replaced with an emptiness. He often wondered if he would ever overcome that emptiness, and that he'd finally have escaped the loop, but she never gave him the chance. Once he was firmly in the midst of lonely despair, past longing for her but not even close to climbing out on his own, then she would appear. It wasn't even on his terms anymore; that was the worst of it. She was completely in control now.

Five Years Earlier

Arthur was prepared this time, bringing more

than a phone and a rucksack full of snacks. Despite this he still felt apprehension as he made his way through the woods. It had been five years since he'd been here. What if the mansion wasn't even there anymore? What if it was, but she wasn't? That was the focus of his return, after all.

It had been an odd five years since collecting the winnings from the lottery ticket. Five million pounds. It had changed his life, of course. No student loan, nice new car, nice house paid for near university. The rest went into a decent savings account, and he lived comfortably off the interest. It should have been the time of his life; all the worries that usually plagued people his age about the future and financial security had been completely removed, after all. And it was; he was happy then. But right from the start, he couldn't quite shake the feeling of Nivian against his skin. He'd been with other women since, but they all seemed lacking compared to her. Like she was more than them but also less, as if everything about her had been compressed into nothing more than the ability to be exactly what he felt he needed at that moment.

He hadn't gone back to the mansion in the past five years. There had been times he had come close, but decided against it. Whatever had happened there-- about which he'd told no-one--he'd had no explanation for it. It was the stuff of fairy tales and fever dreams. That scared him, the fact he'd experienced such a thing and had evidence of its reality forced him to widen his understanding of the world. Going back to the mansion would only reinforce that, and therefore open him up to any possible consequence of that. Up to now the other shoe had never fallen, and he had no desire to test that.

Now, though, something had changed. He wanted to make the highly improbable into reality, and he'd done that once before. If it had been so easy last time, then another visit couldn't hurt, he'd told himself. As the house once again loomed in the clearing, he felt a sense of relief and excitement that quickened his pace. Once inside the door, he fastened some strong cables to the stone wall and then descended into the flooded basement as though he were caving. He wore a headlamp and waterproofs, thick gloves and boots, all of which gave him the feeling of being in control of the situation this time.

That all evaporated the moment he saw her.

"Hello, Arthur." Said Nivian, rising up from the water the moment he touched down in it.

"Nivian, I'm so glad you're here."

"You are? Then give me a hug." She came forward and wrapped her arms around him in an embrace. He shuddered and bit his bottom lip. Everything he'd felt before came screaming back the moment he touched her.

"I'm sorry I haven't come back before now. I know five years is a long time, it's just…"

"Is it?" she interrupted him.

"Is what?"

"Is five years a long time? It didn't feel like it."

"Does time move differently for, um…whatever you are?" Arthur fumbled over his words.

"No, my love. It's just all relative. To a butterfly that lives for a day, a single minute is forever. But to an Oaktree that stands for centuries, it's inconsequential."

"So you're…old?"

"Do I look old, Arthur?" she asked, stepping back and holding her arms out to display herself.

"No, you really don't."

"What is it you think that I am?"

"Beautiful."

"Thank you." She smiled. "But that's not what I meant. You look at a flower; you know it's a flower. You look at a dog; you know it's a dog. You look at me, and you see a woman…but you know that's not all."

"I think you're a water nymph, or a sprite, or a siren or maybe the truth behind all those sort of things."

"My boy is so clever," she purred, pressing closer and gently kissing the nape of his neck. "And you believe that, then?"

"I sort of have to." Arthur blinked a few times, trying to focus on what he was saying as her hand slid down over his chest. "It's not that unusual, really. People once thought giant squids were the stuff of myth until they found one and had it scientifically verified, so…."

He stopped speaking when Nivian placed her mouth over his and forced her tongue inside, sucking the breath from him in a kiss that made him forget the world. When she withdrew, the light from his headlamp caught her eyes, and for a moment they seemed different, almost serpentine.

"What is it you want?" she asked him.

"The last time you said that to me…"

"You got what you asked for?"

"Yes."

"So ask again."

"I want to, but I don't feel right about it. Now

that I'm here with you, to just ask something of you, however it is that you do it, without giving anything in return…"

"You give me plenty in return," she replied, her hand slowly but firmly rubbing over his crotch. He could feel the electricity from her touch even through the waterproof overalls.

"You mean, um, when we…"

"When you fuck me?"

"That's good for you? I mean it's amazing for me, but I didn't know that it was worth anything to you."

"It's worth everything, Arthur," she insisted. "After all, what is the most valuable thing to all that exist? Beyond wealth or jewelry or anything so mundane, what is the priority?"

"Love?"

Nivian laughed, then squeezed his crotch. "Sustenance. For you it's food and water, for me it's the energy released when I…well, I think you can figure out the rest."

"Oh! You, um, feed on that?"

"In a manner of speaking."

"Then do you go out into the world? To find it. You can't struggle to find someone, looking like you do."

"Once upon a time I did, but now I stay here."

"Do you need me to come here more often? I mean, if it's sustenance…"

"You're very sweet. I like that. And of course I would like to see you more often. How could I not? The world is different now, for me and the outside. When I would go out into the world I could find many lonely men and women to lay with."

"Women, too?"

"Does that surprise you?"

"No, it just didn't occur to me."

"You like the thought, though, don't you?" She grinned, her hand starting to move again. "Me laying with another female. Or two."

"Yeah, it's...um..." He was struggling with words now.

"So tell me Arthur...what is it that you want?" She ceased her hand movement again so he could gather enough words to answer.

"The money I won...I've put most of it into a new software company. It's struggling; I think I messed up. I want it to do well. Amazingly well. For me, for everyone else who works there."

"You want its fortunes to ever rise, and yours along with it?"

"Yes."

"Done."

Present Day.

"Is everything alright, Arthur?" asked his mother, staring at him from across the table.

"Hm? Oh yes, sorry. My mind was just elsewhere," Arthur replied, realizing now that he must have been sitting and staring at his food for quite some time without taking a mouthful.

"Anywhere interesting?" his father asked.

"No, just work stuff." Arthur forced a smile, taking a mouthful of his food.

This was a lie, of course. He didn't think about work, he didn't have to. Following his wish to Nivian that the company's fortunes would improve, a series of successful mergers had taken it to undreamed-of heights. The annual profits were beyond anything Arthur had ever thought might be possible, and his own take-home as CEO dwarfed his initial lottery win year on year. The stronger the company had got, the less he had needed to do.

To many this would sound ideal, but this was far from the case for Arthur. Without anything pressing to occupy his thoughts, they would turn back to Nivian. Her scent, her look, the feel of her skin. It was insane really; he knew it was. Time with her was never more than an hour at best, usually far less given the physical effect she had on him. He couldn't reconcile with himself how it could possibly make sense to spend so much time thinking about a one hour slot of time.

This wasn't love, he knew that. It wasn't even lust, but much closer to obsession. Those moments with her were all he felt passion for, the only time he didn't feel empty. Yet each time they were together, it made the aftermath even worse. She'd give him everything for an hour, then leave him feeling nothing for weeks as a result. Logic told him it wasn't worth it, of course it wasn't. But he couldn't stop.

Two Years Ago

"Nivian?" Arthur called as he descended into the mansion basement. He was once again kitted out with the caving gear, but this time he felt far less in control. He was shaking, but not from fear of what he might find. This time it was from fear he might not find what he was looking for.

"I'm here, my love." Nivian appeared as she always did, rising silently from the water.

"I'm so glad to see you." Arthur embraced her.

"How long has it been this time?"

"Three years."

"Not as long as last time, then. You weren't tempted to come back before?"

"Constantly, but I've been really busy with the company and everything."

"So you think of me, then?" asked Nivian.

"I always think of you."

"Do you think of me whilst you pleasure yourself?"

"Yes," Arthur admitted.

"Whilst you're with other women?"

"Yes," Arthur admitted.

"Then in a way you never left me." She smiled, cuddling herself up to his chest and resting her head against it. "What is it you're here for?"

"I'm sick, Nivian."

"Sick?"

"It's called cancer, it's a disease. There are treatments, but…"

"I know what cancer is, lover."

"It's not looking good, Nivian. I'm alright at the moment, but once it really gets aggressive I'm going to decline fast."

"Are you asking me to heal you?"

"Can you do that?"

"I can't lay hands on you and heal you, no. But I can do what I always do; affect probabilities so that your cancer goes into full remission by itself."

"You can?"

"And I will."

Arthur burst into tears. "Thank you, thank you so much."

"Shh, it's alright. You don't need to be scared

anymore; I'm here." Nivian held herself close to him.

"I assume you still want to, um…"

"Don't you?"

"You know I do."

Nivian kissed him, drawing blood from his lip with her teeth.

"I must seem so feeble to you, I guess you don't have to worry about this kind of thing." Arthur shrugged, pausing for a moment.

"I'm not invulnerable to harm, Arthur. I've walked through fire, but I can burn. I live in the water but I can drown. If someone wishes me harm then they can cause it."

"I'd never let anyone hurt you," Arthur said, brushing a strand of wet red hair from her face.

"My brave knight. You would protect me, would you?"

"If it was in my power, then yes. Of course."

"Could you love me, Arthur?" she asked, looking up at him and staring so deeply into his eyes that he could feel her in his soul.

"I…"

"I understand," she turned away from him, covering her chest and appearing vulnerable for the first time since Arthur had met her. "I'm a creature that lives in a dark hole. You see me once every few years. How could you love me?"

"I could. I think I probably already do," Arthur assured her, standing behind her and putting his arms around her waist. She leaned into him and breathed softly.

"It won't always be like this. I'm getting stronger," Nivian said, stroking her long fingernails up his arm.

"That's wonderful."

Nivian turned and looked up at him. "Tell me what you want, Arthur," she said as she leapt up and wrapped her legs around his waist.

"I want my cancer to be gone."

"Done."

Twenty Months Ago

The piece of paper in Arthur's hands seemed so light that it might float away at any time. He knew what it said before he even opened it, but he'd asked for written confirmation. To his mind that somehow made it more real, and he wanted this as real as possible. Full Remission, All Clear. The four greatest words he'd ever read. He needed to call Lance, and his parents. He could text them all at once, but that seemed a bit cold. Something like this needed to be said with a human voice. There was a knock at the door, and Arthur jumped up to answer it. Whoever it might be he'd probably tell them his news, he couldn't help himself.

"Hello lover," Nivian said, standing in the doorway as Arthur opened the door. "Did you miss me?" Nivian was dressed for the first time since Arthur had known her. Her hair was dry, hanging loose and wavy over her shoulders. She was wearing a black corset with a black leather skirt, fishnet tights and black boots.

"Nivian?" Arthur almost did a double take. "How…"

"I told you you were making me stronger. I can leave there now, so I thought I'd come visit you. How are you feeling?" she asked, although Arthur suspected she already knew the answer.

"I'm great, better than great. I'm fine. Which is thanks to you."

"Are you going to ask me in?"

"Oh, is it like a vampire thing? Do you need to be invited?"

"No, I'm being polite," she said with a smile.

"Come in, welcome to my home." Arthur stepped back and let her walk by him. Even clothed she was the most captivating thing he'd ever seen. He couldn't take his eyes off her.

"It's nice to be so high above the earth, after being under it for so long," Nivian remarked, taking a seat on Arthur's couch. He watched as she crossed one leg over the other, the leather skirt riding up her perfect thighs. She didn't pull it back down.

"Can I ask you something?" said Arthur as he joined her on the couch. He sat on the opposite end to her, suddenly feeling awkward around her. She was out of context for him now. She'd escaped the dream bubble of the flooded basement and come straight into his reality.

"You can ask me anything."

"Why the rock chick look?"

"Don't you like it?"

"I like it a lot. I just wonder…I mean, did you *know* I'd like it? Did you take that out of my head?" "It wasn't exactly your head doing the thinking." Nivian smiled at him. "But yes, I knew. You can dress me however you like."

"That's good to know." Arthur blushed.

"You're thinking about bending me over this couch right now, aren't you?"

"I, um…"

"Tearing the fishnets open at the back once

you've raised my skirt?"

"Are you actually psychic?"

She shook her head. "Perceptive."

~/~

For the next year or so, Arthur saw Nivian all the time. He went on what he termed 'proper' dates with her, taking her to restaurants, films, the theatre. All of which ultimately proved pointless. Whenever they were together, he couldn't think of anything excepting wanting to be inside her. Which she was always more than willing to oblige, of course. He no longer even asked her to grant any reality-altering desires afterwards. To climax with her was prize enough now.

After a few months, they gave up even the pretense of dates, and she would simply turn up for them to have sex. At one point Arthur's company advertised for a new intern, and she turned up at the interview. Given that the interview was conducted by Arthur and a colleague of his, Arthur had to feign ignorance through the entire procedure, trying to remain professional. Trying to pay attention to the (surprisingly good) answers she gave to the questions, trying not to stare at her. She'd tied her hair back, worn a smart shirt and tight business skirt, the top of her black stockings ever-so-slightly visible as she sat down. She knew that he was looking, and he knew that she knew. As soon as the interview was over, whilst 'walking her out', Arthur had found a quiet office and bent her over the photocopier. She'd got the job, of course, meaning he could now sleep with her at work, as well.

It was when he missed his mother's birthday that

Arthur realized he had a problem. The family had always been close. Not 'unusually' close, but the sort of close where birthdays were always a cause for them to gather and have dinner. Arthur had not only missed the day itself, but he'd forgotten to even get a present or card. It had entirely slipped his mind, full as it was with nothing but thoughts of Nivian.

"I think I need to see you a little less than I do," he'd said, thinking it would be as easy as that.

"You need me," Nivian replied.

"There's nothing else I want. I haven't even asked for anything since…"

"Not for that. You have the life of your dreams now, it's true. But you don't care about any of it. All you think of is me. All that gives you meaning, is me. You can't just start to limit that, Arthur."

"I can. I'm sorry Niv, but I have to."

Present Day

He had tried, of course. Thinking back on the past few months, trying to be apart from Niv had occupied most of his waking hours. He'd gone into work when there was no need, gone on dates with women whose names he couldn't even remember, and thrown increasingly elaborate parties. It was all just white noise though, forced into the background by his all-consuming thoughts of her. When would he see her again, touch her again. The thoughts of her, the desire for her, had infected every aspect of his life. And each time he started to feel like he might be getting better, she'd come back and remind him what he was denying himself.

Arthur had contemplated speaking to Lance more than once, but always decided against it. All

Lance knew about the situation was that Arthur had visited an allegedly haunted house back in their university days, and whilst there he'd fallen into a flooded basement. That was it, the extent to which he'd shared his tale in one mildly amusing anecdote. Perhaps he could try again, he thought. His mobile phone was on the coffee table in front of him, next to the empty bottle of vodka and the pain pills he'd been taking. Nothing was particularly wrong with him, physically at least, but the pills brought about a kind of numbness he relished. Combined with the vodka, it took the edge off thoughts of Nivian.

She swam in his head again the moment his thoughts touched upon her name. Arthur closed his eyes tightly and shook his head, then snatched up his phone and dialed a number.

"What's up, mate? Not having another shit party already are you?"

"No, I…I need to see you."

"Are you alright?"

"No. No, I'm not. I need your help."

"Right, give me ten minutes."

The tone in Lance's voice was clear; concern mixed with determination. Hearing it made Arthur feel strong for a moment. Somebody cared. Enough to drop everything and come round exactly when they were needed. A sliver of hope appeared in Arthur's mind, that perhaps Lance might just be enough. He couldn't shake her off alone, he just knew it. But with help from a friend? That might prove a different story.

~/~

"It looks like it'd be haunted." Lance remarked as he walked beside Arthur. The old decrepit mansion lay before them, appearing unchanged and untouched since the last time Arthur had seen it.

"It isn't haunted, technically. Not by a ghost. And she's not even here now; she left."

"So what is she, again? A succubus?"

"I think she's a siren, or a nymph."

"Succubi are the ones that shag you and drain the life energy, right?"

"Yeah, so?"

"So, that sounds like your little girlfriend to me."

"She hasn't drained the life out of me," Arthur protested.

"You sure? Not physically perhaps, but mentally she has. I wondered if you were on drugs or something, with how distant you always seem lately, but it's her. She's taken something from you and got her hooks in."

"I don't know what she is, or whether it's even something we can explain. I know it sounds like I'm mental, but…"

"If I thought that I wouldn't be here, mate." Lance patted his friend on the shoulder. "I don't know what this bird is about, where she comes from or how she does what she does to you. But you asked me for help, so I'm here. I'm just treating this like I would if you said you'd got a gambling problem or whatever. If I think too much about the specifics, then my head wants to melt."

"Fair enough." Arthur smiled.

"Fucking weird though, isn't it? To think some of this mythological shit might be real?"

"It doesn't mean *everything* is. That's false logic.

Just because we discovered there might be some truth to one sort of mythical creature doesn't mean the Loch Ness monster and Bigfoot and everything else must be real."

"I know, but it makes me think about how these stories start. There's got to be a grain of truth to them somewhere back in history." Lance shrugged. "Anyway, sorry. You're probably not wanting a discussion about this now."

"Actually, it helps. Partly because it distracts me, but also it makes her more real. Talking about this, it gives a form to her, stops her being this ethereal thing that only I know about."

"I saw her at your party, mate. She's real enough."

"Well, that's also reassuring."

"Tits to die for, too."

"Not helping, Lance."

"Sorry. More seriously, then, what's your plan here? We've spoken about everything that's happened, but not what you're going to do next. Or even why we're actually here at her house."

"This isn't her house. I've always known that, really; it's just hard to articulate thoughts about her into a logical pattern."

"This is where you found her though, right? So whose house is it?" asked Lance.

"I don't know, but that's not the point. Whoever lived in that house, however long ago it was, must have had a relationship with her too. And when it got too much, they found a way to trap her."

"Trap her?"

"She couldn't leave when I found her. It was only after I'd given her enough strength that she was able to. But to start, she just had to wait for me there. In that basement. I don't think that was by choice."

"So, her previous lover managed to trap her in the basement and then fuck off and leave her there for centuries, or however long? And you think the knack to how he did it is still in that house?"

"I've no idea. It might be. But I've got to try. I can't just quit her. She won't stop coming to me. It's like a drug with a consciousness, with its own will. Every day you wake up wanting to be clean, and there's a syringe waiting on your bedside table. I need to force her to stop coming to me. That's the only way I'm going to be able to get free."

"You could kill her," Lance offered with a shrug.

"Seriously?" said Arthur with a frown.

"She's not human."

"No, but she's a conscious living entity. We can't just murder her."

"But trapping her in a basement again is alright?"

"If we start going into the morals of this, we'll never get anywhere. Let's just go inside."

The two entered the house. Arthur showed Lance how to fasten the climbing cables to the stone wall, and they began the descent into the hole.

"We should do things like this more often," Lance suggested, earning him a frown from Arthur. He went on. "Not specifically this. I mean getting out, doing things. It gets you out of your head."

"It does; you're right. I always feel better when I'm not just sat by myself. Alright, this water's going to be cold, so brace yourself," Arthur suggested as they lowered themselves down the breach in the floor.

"There's no water." Lance remarked, angling his

headlamp downwards.

"It must have drained somehow."

"Also, check out that shit." Lance took a hand from his ropes to point at the large pentagram that was painted on the floor of the basement. Arthur had never noticed it before, given the volume of murky water that had previously covered it.

"Wonder if that's how he trapped her?" Arthur suggested.

The two of them came to a gentle landing on the basement floor. Patches of moss were visible on the concrete, and on closer inspection the pentagram was only one of many symbols painted beneath their feet. Some of them were familiar from horror films and videogames, but he had no clue as to their actual meaning. Pop culture was hardly a trustworthy source for such things. Both men shone their headlamps over the symbols, studying them as though increased lighting might somehow make their meaning more obvious.

"They're not broken." Arthur remarked.

"What do you mean?"

"The symbols. They're not broken or damaged or anything. Nivian told me she'd gotten strong enough to escape now, but the symbols aren't damaged. So, what changed? How did she get out?"

"What else is different? Was she in chains or something before?"

"No, she seemed free to move around in…the water." Arthur snapped his fingers and grabbed Lance by the shoulders. "The water, Lance! It wasn't her home; that was her prison! Or part of it, at least."

"I thought she was a water creature?"

"So did I, because I found her in it. But maybe

not. I mean think about it, what if all those stories of people finding these creatures in water sources go that way because the creature was already imprisoned somehow?"

"You mean some old warrior blokes, like Conan or something, went round locking these nymphs in bodies of water to keep them from mischief? But horny travelers found them anyway?"

"Ooh, your friend is clever," Nivian purred, her voice seeming to echo from all around the basement.

"Niv…" Arthur swallowed the icy lump in his throat as he watched her appear from the shadows. Once again, she was entirely naked.

"What are you boys here for? It's not a nice place to visit," she said, circling them like cat. "And Arthur, if you wanted to bring a friend to play, I'm sure your big, soft bed would be nicer than this cellar."

"That's not why we're here, Niv." Arthur replied.

Lance backed away slowly, alternately keeping his eye on Niv and glancing around the room for the source of the previous flooding. In the far corner, he spotted an old iron pipe. It was thick, probably the mains, he thought. There was a folded part in the middle where the metal had been crushed over an existing split in the pipe. Lance imagined the previous owner had taken an axe to it to create the flood, and Niv had crushed the pipe to seal the leak once she was strong enough. Crushed a metal pipe by hand. How strong was she? As these thoughts haunted his mind, Lance also noticed that Niv looked slightly different than he remembered her. She was still beautiful, but she seemed slightly less human now. Her eyes were dark, looking almost reptilian. She seemed to shimmer, and when the faint light from above caught her skin, it even seemed to have pale greenish scales.

"I can't see you anymore, Niv." said Arthur, feeling guilty despite himself.

"So you've said before. But you don't send me away when I come, do you?"

"I wasn't strong enough. But I mean it this time."

"They always say that." Nivian laughed mockingly.

"I'm not doing it alone, now."

"Oh yes, your special friend, Lance. Your only actual friend who knows the real you, not the false version I crafted." Her tone was severe, cutting.

"I just need to move on. I don't blame you, I know you only did what I asked. This was my fault, but that means it's my choice to end it."

"You think you can just trap me here again, is that it?"

"Not if I believed you'd leave me alone."

"We both know that's not what you really want." Nivian slipped close to Arthur, running her hands over his body. He responded to her touch immediately, his blood diving south. "You just want me to fuck you...here where it started...don't you?"

"I..." Arthur felt his will leaving him at her touch. "I do...but..."

"Arthur!" Lance yelled from the corner of the room. He had found a broken piece of iron railing from a long-decayed staircase and was using it to re-open the gash in the water pipe. "You're not shagging some bird whilst I'm stood in the same room, mate. Sorry."

With that, Lance pushed his body weight onto

the broken railing and ripped the pipe open. Water gushed out at a higher velocity than he'd been expecting, which both pushed him back and also collided with Niv and Arthur with enough impact to knock them off their feet. Arthur was winded, coughing and shaking his head to clear his vision. As he moved to stand back up, Niv was on top of him, holding him down to the ground by his wrists.

"You like when I'm on top, don't you, lover?" she hissed, her tongue now leaving her lips and appearing distinctly serpentine as it stretched down impossibly far to lick Arthur's face.

Nivian now looked even less human than she did before. Her entire body was covered in shiny, pale green scales. Her hands were elongated claws, her eyes undeniably reptilian. She held Arthur down with a single hand and began to tear open his clothes as the water rose steadily higher around them.

"Clever boy, figuring out the fact that you needed the water to keep me here," said Nivian, licking his now-exposed chest. "But it won't do you any good. I'm strong enough now that it'll only take one fuck to get out again. Just one. But maybe I'll take Lance, too, as dessert. I'm a hungry girl, I won't lie."

"Not bloody likely." Lance announced, striking Niv around the back of the head with the iron rod.

The blow knocked her off Arthur, whose face was now submerged beneath the water. Lance dragged him to his feet, and the two instinctively went back to back.

"Where the fuck is she?" asked Lance, realizing Niv was now nowhere in sight.

As if in answer, a dozen scaly tentacles rose up

around them, lashing out like snakes striking. Lance knocked a couple away with the rod, then one wrapped itself around the weapon and snatched it away. The tentacles shimmered and altered, each becoming Niv, but each slightly different. Some blonde, some brunette, some with her the more familiar red hair.

"Come on, boys, let's not make this unpleasant." The cast of Nivians spoke in eerie unison.

"Surrounded by hot naked women, and I'm not happy about it. What have you done to my life, Arthur?" Lance joked, trying to mask the panic in his voice.

"You're really annoying sometimes, just so you know," Arthur replied.

The multiple Nivians were surrounding them now, their hands all over the both of them. Clearly it no longer mattered which of them they took, she just needed one more carnal act to regain her freedom. The hands were as busy trying to remove Lance's clothing now as they were Arthur's, and this fact brought a realization to Arthur's mind. Her hold on him wasn't as strong, and more importantly, she knew it.

"We're done, Niv. We are fucking done!" Arthur roared, grabbing Lance and pushing past the gathered Nivians in a rugby charge.

Tentacles snatches at their ankles beneath the water once again, making Arthur wonder what on earth Nivian's true form actually was, but they kept moving.

"Here, quick." Arthur passed the rope to Lance and gave him a boost up, then grabbed his own and started climbing. He was a few feet up when a hand grabbed his ankle.

"I thought you loved me," Niv said, looking up at him pleadingly. She looked human again now, for the moment.

"No, Niv, I'm sorry," he replied, snatching his ankle away and climbing up the rope as quickly as he could.

Arthur and Lance reached the ground floor and ran for the door, unhooking their ropes and leaving as fast as they could. Nivian roared behind them, an inhuman wail that shook the mansion to its foundations. Once they were a safe distance away, both men stopped and hunched over their knees, catching their breath as best they could.

"That was mental," Lance said.

"Yeah. Sorry."

"Hey, as long as you're alright. I can process it later."

"I am, I think. I mean, I feel like I will be."

"You're not alone, though, mate. Not now."

"No. I should have thought about that before."

"Can see why you'd get lost in her so easily, though. The way it feels when she touches you…"

"Let's not talk about that, alright?" Arthur asked.

"Alright, but it's hardly the first time we've got felt up by the same bird. Remember that hippy in college who…"

"Lance!"

"Fine, shutting up," Lance huffed. "What are we doing next week, then? Killing a dragon? Finding some buried treasure?"

"Let's start with a drink."

Epilogue.

The lone visitor entered the mansion, carefully hooking his rope to the stone wall. The previous visitors had left hooks in it already, but he didn't trust to re-use the same ones, applying a new one just in case. Once satisfied he was secure, the visitor slowly descended into the hole. He shuddered slightly at the touch of the cold water as he reached the bottom. From his back pocket, the visitor took a torch and scanned the room around him.

"Hello? Nivian?" he called.

The water didn't move, not disturbed in the slightest, but a pale, beautiful figure rose behind him. She smiled, and wrapped her arms around his waist.

"Hello Lance."

Bloody Mary

Michael Bernstein

from storm-torn plains and crumbled peaks, I invoke
      you
from barren earth and venom seas, I invoke you
from pillaged cities and fouled shines, I invoke you
with profane rites in arcane tongues, I invoke you
for pleasure in the spill of blood, I invoke you
for vengeance of the Left Hand sought, I invoke you

from fathoms lost to light of day, I invoke you
from horizons of ceaseless graves, I invoke you
from eons in the frozen core, I invoke you
from your banishment from Form, I invoke you

I invoke you!
I invoke you!
I invoke you!

www.ingramcontent.com/pod-product-compliance
Lightning Source LLC
Chambersburg PA
CBHW051503170626
46811CB00002B/629